VAMPIRES OR GODS?

by

William Meyers

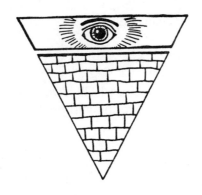

III Publishing
P.O. Box 170363
San Francisco, CA 94117-0363

1st Printing: September 1993

Cover Design by William Meyers

ISBN 0-9622937-5-X

TABLE OF CONTENTS

5

Introduction

"Mind you do not slip, for the road behind and ahead is wet with blood. Man-robbers are now more numerous than gold-robbers. If they are intent of robbing people of reason and awareness, what then will they make of him who is unaware of himself?"
— Jalal Al-din Rumi

The Reality of Immortality

The vampire is immortal. The vampire defies death. The vampire can give the gift, or curse, of immortality to other men and women. That is the essence of the vampire "myth."

Some religious adherents insist that their God lives, today, in human form, but immortal. Many past religions insisted that their God lived and claimed immortality for him. Only a few religious systems, notably Judaism, Islam, and some forms of Buddhism, worship an abstract God that has no divine, immortal, human counterpart on earth.

The materialistic, naturalistic (and sometimes atheistic) world-view that developed in Europe in this millennium rejected all these claims. Most scholars went so far as to deny that immortal religious figures like Hercules, Romulus, Osiris and Jesus Christ ever had a real existence. They claimed that these figures were mythological creations of the human imagination. In particular, since the Christians had already convinced most people that Greek, Roman, and other gods were mythological, scholars wrote many a book trying to

Egyptian Mummy. Preservation of the body was closely
associated with the vampire cult of Isis and Osiris and
the hope for physical resurrection. Rosicrucian Museum,
San Jose.

convince people that Jesus Christ either never existed or, if he did exist, did not rise from the dead.

But scientists today are beginning to make immortality imaginable even for those of us born mortal. A recent Scientific American article surveying publicly known research [Why Do We Age? by Ricki L. Rusting, December, 1992, p. 130] offers a variety of experimental ways of extending life well into a second century. Most important, research verifies that there is a strong genetic component to longevity: each species of life has a basic life-span, within which is some degree of variation.

Perhaps the ancient Gods, including those discussed in this book, were merely exceptionally endowed men and women. Perhaps they lived to be 120 in an age when living to be 40 was unusual. Or perhaps they lived far longer; some may be alive today, two millennia or more after their births.

Later chapters will focus on the historical record. What I say here must remain, at present, speculation: a consideration of possibilities. This book will focus on those men and women claiming to have been humans who somehow triumphed over death. I cannot claim to say much about vampires in general: perhaps only a few have tried, or been successful, at setting themselves up as gods. If there were more immortals, perhaps they found life to be better posing as businessmen, or as bums, rather than posing as gods or sages. But to look for vampires in the historical record, they must be in it; and religious cults of sufficient size tend to show up in the history books.

The Resurrection of the Dead

Consider one definition of a vampire: "a corpse that becomes reanimated" [Webster's New World Dictionary]. In most of the cases of beings claiming to be Gods presented in this book, Godhood came only after death. Therefore it is often assumed that immortality was in the spirit, not in the flesh. Those who deny that vampires exist claim that "the spirit" was memories of the living, perhaps in dreams or a result of temporary schizophrenia. When Krishna, Orpheus, or the Blessed Virgin Mary appears to someone in our present time, the skeptics again call it a hallucination or dream.

8

Silver Chalice. Possibly used in Christian ceremonies of the 2nd Century A.D. to drink wine — or blood. From the tomb of a bishop at Riha, Syria.

Many people, however, maintain that the spirit is something separable from the body. They might argue that since a voice can be sent by radio waves, and a computer's intelligence stored on a magnetic tape, perhaps some medium exists that supports human consciousness, apart from the brain. In that case, presumably, longevity or immortality would rest on the nature of the medium and the coherence of the mind and personality.

But against this whole theory is the plain claim that the corpses of the ancient gods were, in fact, reanimated. Skeptics claim that, since reanimation is impossible, either they were not really, totally dead, or those with a stake in the nascent religion hid the dead body and lied about it. Certainly in ancient times, as in the present day, some people came so close to death that those who observed them genuinely believed they had perished. And certainly men lie, especially when their egos or livelihoods are at risk.

In the world of plants and animals, however, reanimation is a much more common feat. Many animals can regenerate a lost limb or tail as easily as humans can heal a flesh wound. Most children have observed a mosquito or fly that, having been swatted and left for dead, has resurrected itself. Perhaps some humans have that ability.

Then there is the possibility that we are not dealing, in the case of vampire-gods, with humans at all. Perhaps they are a distinct species, related to man as man is related to gorillas. Or the gods were a result of a mating between immortal beings and ordinary humans, as is claimed in the stories of Dionysus, Hercules, Jesus Christ and others. Perhaps the rash of women claiming to have been abducted by UFO's in the past two decades will find that their children are immortal or have unusual abilities.

One informant who claims to know real "vampires," humans who do not age or age only slowly, says that while they are not sure what causes their condition, a common theory is that it is simply a rare and recessive gene or set of genes. This could explain why most immortals chronicled in this book were the result of some sort of sexual liaison that today is considered incest. The most common circumstances were men mating with their female descendants, and sisters mating with their brothers, both of which would tend to make a recessive gene manifest (and in fact usually results not in immortality, but in degeneration). The incestuous relations of the Greek gods are well known, as

No. 79.   SAVED THROUGH JESUS' BLOOD.

J. W. V.   J. W. VanDeVenter.

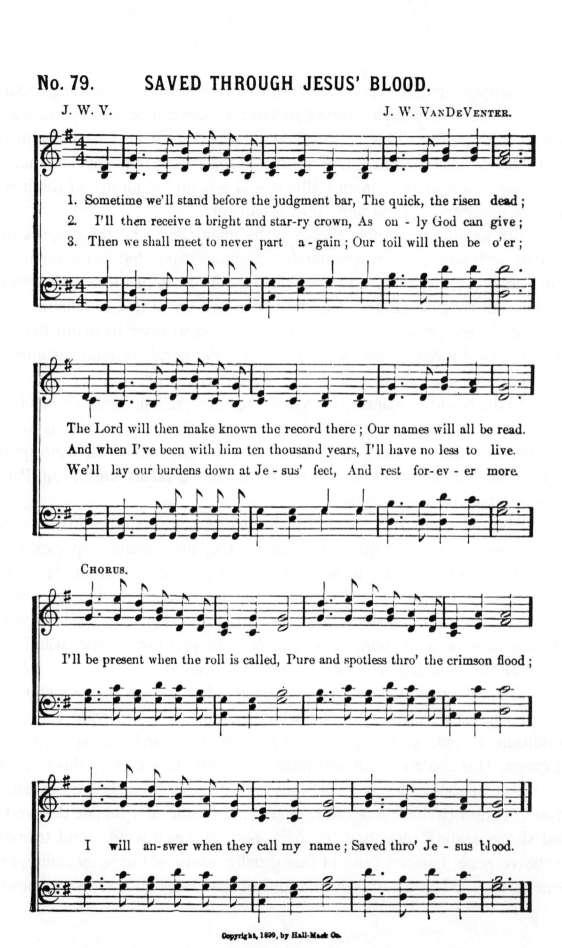

1. Sometime we'll stand before the judgment bar, The quick, the risen **dead**;
2. I'll then receive a bright and star-ry crown, As on - ly God can **give**;
3. Then we shall meet to never part a - gain; Our toil will then be o'er;

The Lord will then make known the record there; Our names will all be **read**.
And when I've been with him ten thousand years, I'll have no less to live.
We'll lay our burdens down at Je - sus' feet, And rest for - ev - er more.

CHORUS.

I'll be present when the roll is called, Pure and spotless thro' the crimson flood;

I will an-swer when they call my name; Saved thro' Je - sus blood.

Vampires in the 20th Century? This song from Christian
Hymns No. 1, ©1899 strongly suggests ongoing worship.

was the habit of the Egyptian pharaohs of marrying their sisters, perhaps modeling themselves on Isis/Osiris/Horus.

Holy Grail or
Night of the Living Dead?

The title of this book is: Vampires or Gods? For the ordinary person, this is the crucial question. One definition of Gods that fits our subjects is "various beings conceived as supernatural, immortal, and having special powers over the lives and affairs of people" [ibid]. However, with the rise of monotheism each religious cult claimed its particular God was the Supreme and only Deity. A Roman or Greek had several Gods to choose from, and might, in good judgement, at one point serve Mars and at another Venus. Modern worshippers usually put all their eggs in one basket.

To believe that rising from the dead is sufficient to be credentialed as the Supreme Being is to put yourself at grave risk. You may not be worshipping a God, but a vampire. The vampire, to preserve its own immortality, is likely to be more interested in your soul or life energy than in mere blood. Or, if vampires have no special spiritual qualities, they may be interested in servants for their worldly empires.

Blood and Wine

Because of the fame of Bram Stoker's novel <u>Dracula</u>, many people are aware of the (perhaps mythological) particular case of a man who rose from the dead: Vlad III, Prince of Wallachia (not Transylvania, though he spent part of his childhood there), also known as Dracula, the son of Dracul (from the Romanian word for Dragon). The idea that vampires drink blood is closely associated with Dracula, whose resurrection from the dead was correctly seen by the Wallachian and Transylvanian peasants (who had been pagans) as directly prefigured by Jesus Christ's meal of blood and human flesh just before his crucifixion.

Dracul and Dracula introduced Catholicism to Wallachia; the Order of the Dragon promised eternal life to those nobles who would forcibly convert

12

VAMPIRES OR GODS?

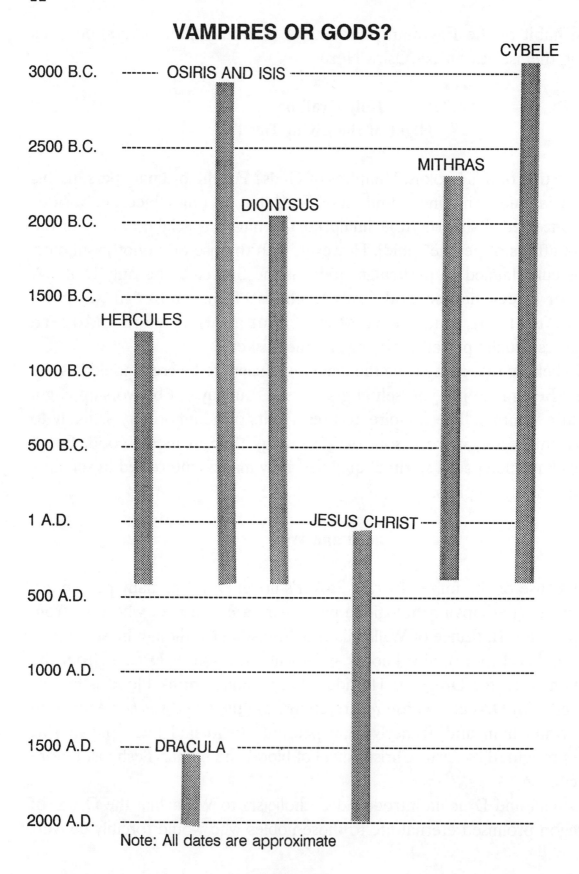

Note: All dates are approximate

TIMELINE

3000 B.C. --

2500 B.C. --

2000 B.C. --

1500 B.C. --

1000 B.C. ------ KRISHNA ----------------------------------

ROMULUS

500 B.C. --

1 A.D. ------------------------------------ QUETZALCOATL

APOLLONIUS   CALIGULA   CHANG LING

500 A.D. --

1000 A.D. --

1500 A.D. --

2000 A.D. --

Note: All dates are approximate

their subjects to Catholicism. Dracula did not claim to be a God. Very likely only a few immortals find that convenient. Instead he went on to be a powerful figure in the Catholic Church, largely responsible for its successful Inquisition in Spain and the conquest of the New World. Rumors abound that to this day he lives in the Vatican and acts as an adviser to the Popes.

However, drinking blood does not appear to be a recipe for immortality. Many people have tried drinking human or animal blood and found that it has no effect upon the aging process. Most of the Immortals examined in this book have no reputation for drinking blood, though a few do. Many, however, (Mithras and Krishna, for example) are warrior Gods who encourage men to spill their blood in battle. And others such as Dionysus and Jesus were closely associated with drinking wine.

Others derived their resurrection from the powers of their wife or mother. Before the Roman/Greek era female gods were perhaps commoner than male gods, but little written material remains from that epoch. Cybele is one woman who was believed to have achieved immortality after starting as a human; this was attributed to her baptism in the blood of a bull.

Fangs, Bats & Etc.

I should say a word about fangs. Movie vampires always have them. None of the vampires discussed in this book, not even Prince Dracula, were depicted with fangs before or after death. The most natural source of this idea is, of course, the need to break the skin to drink blood; for which the fangs of various carnivorous animals doubtless served as models. But the mythical aspect is better served by the association of many vampire-gods, especially Dionysus, with fanged snakes.

Bats are now associated with vampires, and not just through Dracula. There are the infamous vampire bats of South America that bite cattle and then lick up the blood with their tongues. But they are not immortal. Very likely the fact that bats spread rabies, which seems to cause a demonic frenzy in humans, contributed to this myth. Many of the vampire-gods were associated with animals, but none with bats. Jesus Christ could appear as a dove (though more often he was called the Lamb of God) and Quetzalcoatl was also represented as a bird/snake.

Even the lowly mosquitoes and biting flies probably contributed to current vampire-lore. But the purpose of this book is not to attempt to dispel every accreted article of myth, but to clarify the central truths about the vampire-gods.

I would not claim that all immortals are inherently evil. There is much evidence that some immortals dislike the exploitation of mortal humans by their unscrupulous brethren. Claims abound of the many ways some immortals have helped humans. But this may be the ancient, vampire's equivalent of modern corporate advertising campaigns. Hypocrisy has always had a field day in the religious domain. Vampires may care no more for humans than many humans care for animals.

I have put forward many ideas in this short introduction. I believe it is important for people to examine the evidence for themselves, and form their own conclusions. In fact, this entire book can only introduce the topic. Many of our immortals have had volumes written about them, and many men and women claiming to be gods have been ignored herein because of a poverty of information about them. Hopefully those who want to pursue the subject further will find the list of sources at the end of each chapter helpful, as well as the general references at the end of this book.

"Paranoia is knowing what is really going on."
— William S. Burroughs

King Mycerinus of Egypt, builder of the Third Pyramid,
IVth Dynasty, shown alive around 2600 B.C., with Isis and
Nephthys, who were at least 500 years old at that time.

OSIRIS & ISIS

Osiris is the most ancient immortal of whom there is record. We can trace his rise from approximately just before or during the first dynasty of the ancient Egyptians – about 3100 B.C. He was still a powerful vampire-god until at least 400 A.D. Osiris was originally the king of a small city-state, and after his death and resurrection became the central figure of Egyptian religion and perhaps the true power behind the long procession of kingly dynasties.

Archeological evidence shows that religion was well developed in Egypt long prior to the first dynasty. It included a belief in a supreme god almighty whose actions on earth were carried out by lesser gods who were worshipped in their own rites. Pre-dynastic Egyptians saw all sorts of natural objects as dwelling places of the gods; they wore amulets to protect them from evil and were buried in them; believed sacrifices were the highest form of worship; and believed in reward and punishment.

Osiris had been king of Abydos in Upper Egypt. After his death and resurrection he and his priests made their cult popular by promoting the ideals of morality, justice and righteousness, while promising immortality to their followers. People were able to identify with the human aspect of his nature, while hoping to follow his ascent, if not to divinity, at least to immortality. By the end of the first dynasty his was the most popular religion in all of Egypt.

How much of the legend of Osiris that has come down to us is true, we cannot be sure. That legend has many variations. Among the earliest there is the Heliopolitan Recension, the first known version of the "Per-em-hru," or the Book of the Dead. Even this early version was corrupted by the priests of Heliopolis, who, during the 5th and 6th dynasties, created it out of older

5. Harakhtē. 6. Hathor. 7. Cow-headed Hathor.

8. Harendotes (Horus) 9. Isis. 10. Isis, suckling the infant Horus.

Chief Egyptian gods. All of them may have been vampires, who derived their longevity from a recessive gene brought out by inbreeding.

11. Maat, goddess of
truth.

12. Min; behind is the
curious shrine of
the god.

13. Nephthys.

14. Osiris; behind the god is the fetish
of Emē-wet, god of the dead.

Chief Egyptian gods. Nephthys is the sister of Osiris
and Isis.

writings and their own interpolations. The Book of the Dead expanded with the ages; the Theban Recension characterizing the 18th and 19th dynasties is sometimes taken as the standard, but the book did not stabilize until the Saite Recension in 600 B.C.

It is frequently stated that Classic authors of the Greek and Roman period reported on a cult that was weakening, and that the priests of Osiris in that period could not read ancient Egyptian hieroglyphics. But the truth is that the knowledge was simply a closely guarded secret.

The dogma is that the supreme god, Neter, who was self-created, almighty and eternal, produced two other gods, Shu and Tefnut, who, with Neter, formed the Egyptian trinity. They produced numerous greater and lesser gods, including Keb and Nut, whose children were the mortals Isis, Set, Nephthys and Osiris. Though they were brother and sister, Osiris and Isis married and bore Horus.

Set and Osiris fought constantly, and ultimately Set killed Osiris. It was Isis and Horus who were responsible for the resurrection of Osiris. His ascent into heaven was by the grace of the more powerful Gods. Further along, in the document section, this story will be related by the eminent Greek historian Plutarch (46–120 A.D.), and some (unfortunately more difficult) passages will be given from the ancient Egyptian hieroglyphs.

Was Osiris a god or vampire? What was his relation to other ancient immortals?

It is very likely that Isis, who in the legends became an immortal and god in her own right, was either Osiris's mortal wife/queen or was already immortal when she decided to restore him to life. A female goddess appears beside Osiris on some of the cylinders from Abydos, the birthplace of their cult. Isis and Osiris enter the historical record at about the time that patriarchy was triumphing over matriarchy and that city states were first giving way to nations. In the 5th dynasty, like Osiris, she was regarded as the deified member of a family of human beings, and by the 12th dynasty was identified as the Earth-Mother and Queen of Heaven. By Roman times she was a considerably more important god than Osiris. Like Osiris her cult lasted until Christianity put to death all who would not publicly worship a different immortal.

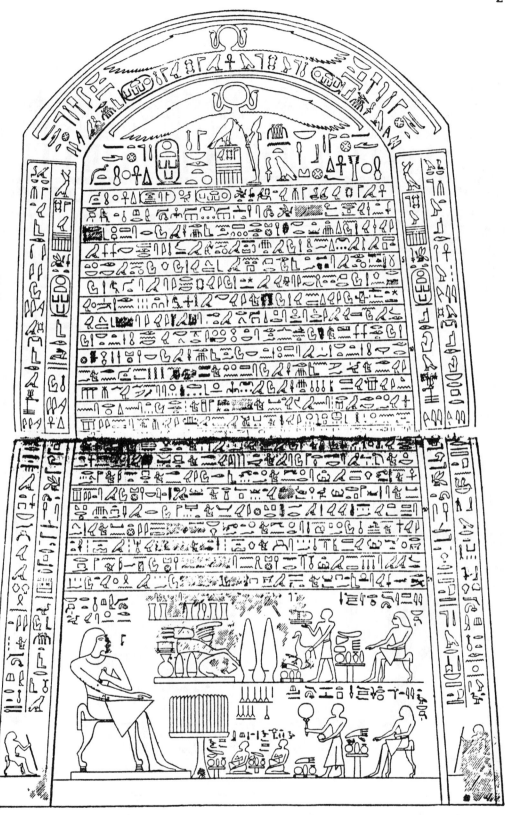

Depiction of memorial stone erected by Royal Treasurer
Ikhernofret around 1900 B.C. at Osiris's sacred city of
Abydos. Records his participation in the Osirian Drama.

From the Papyrus of Hunefer, showing Osiris seated, attended by Nephthys and Isis, with the Eye of Horus in the upper left. British Museum.

The best documentation of Isis comes from the 15th dynasty. Inscriptions from that period tell us that Isis was indeed a woman who was able to resurrect the dead: first restoring a baby to life who had been stung by a scorpion, then restoring her son Horus, who had been murdered by Set; and finally, using secret incantations given her by the god Thoth (or perhaps Ra), resurrecting her long dead husband. She was generally regarded as a great magician. It is important to note that she never died. Therefore she can be regarded as the source-stream of immortality.

Like other vampires, Isis and Osiris were reputed to have appeared to their followers. Whether this was a trick of priests, or whether then appeared in people's minds or actually appeared in the flesh, cannot be said.

Osiris was eventually associated with the bull, and Isis with the cow. Perhaps this is important in relation to Mithras, who was reputed to have slain the bull. Perhaps this is mere analogy to the decline of Egypt's political and economic power, or perhaps the ancient immortals were actually rivals for power who sometimes slew each other.

In relation to vampire legends generally, an important point is that Osiris, when resurrected, was not whole, but had lost his phallus. Vampires are generally conceived of as unable to bear children; Horus was conceived prior to Osiris becoming immortal. Later, however, for obvious reasons it was asserted that Osiris did indeed have a working penis, so that any men resurrected by him might expect that same pleasure.

Regarding the role of blood, there is little to say except that Isis's symbol was a stylization of female sexual organs, and the most potent amulet mentioned in the hieroglyphics was said to contain her blood. Interestingly, the cult of Isis and Osiris is associated with the end of human sacrifice and cannibalism in Egypt. Perhaps, like some other ancient immortals, Osiris's death and resurrection was seen as the ultimate human sacrifice, one that would satisfy the gods for all time.

At death all men were judged by Osiris, who based their mortality or immortality on their righteousness during life. Hence the religion was a powerful reinforcer of both ethics and civil law.

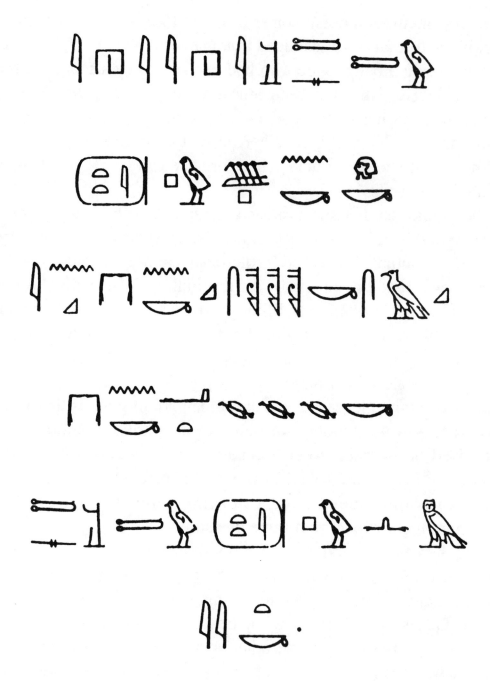

Hieroglyphics from The Book of the Dead of Pepi I. See page 25 for translation.

DOCUMENTS

The Book of the Dead

[from Osiris by E. A. Wallis Budge; most quotes are modernized by the editor; page numbers refer to 1911 Medici Society edition]

p. 69, text of Teta, in which king Teta is identified with Osiris in hopes that, like Osiris, he would be resurrected:

Hail, hail, rise up, Teta! You have received your head, you have embraced your bones, you have gathered together your flesh .... Rise up, thou Teta, thou art not a dead thing.

p. 69-70 similarly in text of Pepi I:

He who comes comes to you, but you move not. Your mother comes to you, you move not. Nut comes to you, you move not. Khnemet-urt comes to you, you move not. She breaths on you, she speaks to you with words of power, you stir. She gives you your head, she presents you your bones, she gathers together your flesh, she brings to you your heart in your body. You are master of your utterances, and you give words of command to those who come before you.

Three selections from the funereal city of Abydos. Upper
left: Cleopatra and Ptolemy on the wall of the Denderah
temple. Upper right: Seti I worshipping Osiris in his
temple. Bottom: The resurrection of Osiris at the temple
of Seti I.

Pyramids and Sphinx. Built in the 3rd Millennia B.C.,
eternal witnesses to the power of Osiris's cult, by then
over 500 years old.

Hail, Osiris Teta, stand up! Horus comes, he has counted you with the gods. Horus loves you! He has filled you with his eye, he has joined his eye to you. Horus has opened his eye that you way see with it. The gods have lifted up your face, they love you. Isis and Nephthys have made you strong. Horus does not depart from you, behold his Ka [double]. He rests on you, and you live. You have received the word of Horus, you rest upon it. Horus hears you, and never fails you. He makes the gods your followers.

Osiris, Teta, rise up! Keb has brought Horus to you, he had called you to life. Horus has found you, he has performed the ceremonies for you. Horus has brought the gods to you, he has given them to you, they illuminate your face. Horus has placed you before the gods, he has made you to take possession of every diadem. Horus has bound them to you, he has not removed them from you... Nephthys has united for you all your body parts in her name of 'Seshat, lady of buildings;' thereby you will be strong. Your mother Nut is given to you in her name of 'Quersut,' she unites you in her name of 'Aar.' Horus presents to you your flesh, he does not place your tomb, he makes you into a complete being, there is no confusion in your life. Horus causes you to rise up unsupported.

p. 44-45: The Book of Making the Spirit of Osiris (from a papyrus of unknown origin)

The formula for making the spirit of Osiris in Akertet, which shall by recited for this god, the Lord of Abydos, at every festival of Osiris, and at every appearance of the god in the temples... It shall make glorious his soul, it shall establish his body, it shall make his soul shine in the sky, and shall make him renew his youth each month, it shall establish his son Horus upon his coffer. This formula was recited by the Sister of Osiris. It will benefit a man if

The Eye of Horus, Osiris's son, from the Papyrus of
Hunefer, with Hieroglyphic Text.

The resurrection of Osiris Khenti-Åmenti.
Mariette, *Dendêrah*, IV, 90.

The resurrection of Osiris.

he recites it, for he shall become a favored one of Osiris upon earth among the living; his son shall be established in his house every day, and his children upon the earth. This formula was recited by Isis and her sister Nephthys, and also by her son Horus. If it is recited for Osiris, it will cause the soul of the deceased to live in Akertet every day, it will gladden his heart, and will overthrow all his enemies. It shall be recited during the 4th month of the season Akhet, from the 22nd day to the 25th day thereof.

Come into your house, come into your house, Oh An. Come to your house, Oh beautiful Bull, the Lord of men and women, the beloved one, the lord of women. O beautiful face, chief of Akertet, prince, first of those who are in the other world, are not all hearts drunk through love of thee?

...

Hail, Osiris Khenti-Amentiu, the gods and the goddesses, with their heads on their knees, await your coming to them: men cry and shout out: 'Oh, invisible one, come to us.' Oh Soul, perfect to all eternity, your members are in a state of well-being, your sufferings are relieved, every evil thing is done away with. Your limbs are rejoined, you are protected, you have no defect. Your limbs are rejoined, and not a member of yours is wanting.

1.   Hail, Osiris Khenti-Amentiu! Oh form, you have your head, god of the lifted hand, your crown and hair are genuine lapis lazuli.

2.   Hail, Osiris Khenti-Amentiu! Oh form, you have your two eyes, you see with them; the Maati goddesses love to protect you.

3.   Hail, Osiris Khenti-Amentiu! Oh form, you have your ears, wherewith you hear prayers for millions of years.

4.   Hail, Osiris Khenti-Amentiu! Oh form, you have your nose, your nostrils smell the breezes.

5.   Hail, Osiris Khenti-Amentiu! Oh form, you have your mouth and speak with it; Horus has pressed it for you.

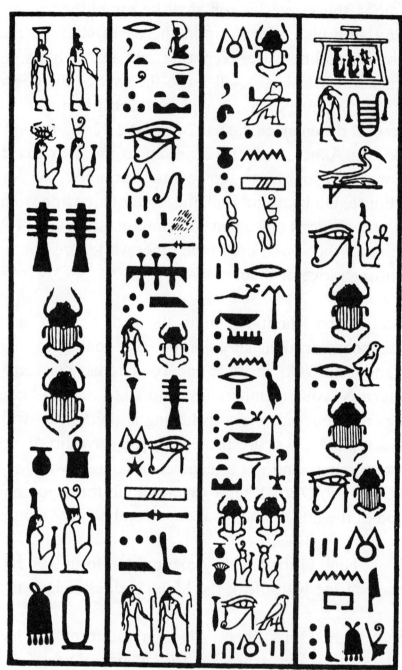

The 104 amulets of Osiris.
Mariette, *Dendérah*, IV, 87.

The Amulets of Osiris. These offered magical protection
and invoked good luck.

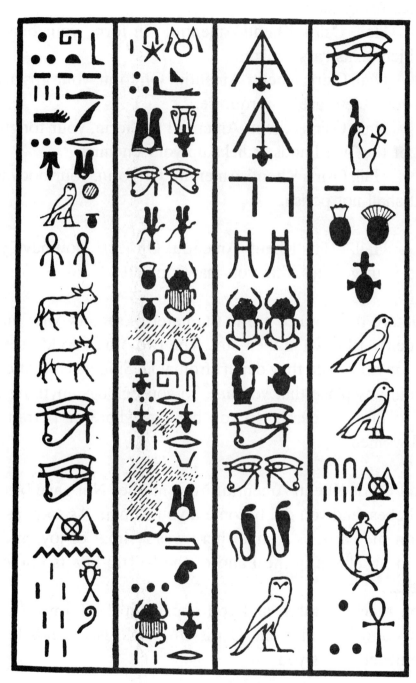

The 104 amulets of Osiris.
Mariette, *Dendérah*, IV, 87.

More Amulets of Osiris.

6.   Hail, Osiris Khenti-Amentiu! Oh form, your jaw-bones are on you, firmly fixed.

7.   Hail, Osiris Khenti-Amentiu! Oh form, your beard is crystal which emits rays of light.

8.   Hail, Osiris Khenti-Amentiu! Oh form, your lips are of flint and your teeth are of turquoise.

9.   Hail, Osiris Khenti-Amentiu! Oh form, your tongue is the pilot of the Two Lands, it licks up your enemies.

10.   Hail, Osiris Khenti-Amentiu! Oh form, your body is of natron, it shall not perish.

...

16.   Hail, Osiris Khenti-Amentiu! Oh form, you have your penis and your genitals, that you may copulate.

...

You are the Lord of Truth, the hater of sinners, who makes them to be overthrown in their sins. The two Maati goddesses are with you, on no day do they depart from you. Sinners cannot come near you in any place that you are. To you belongs anything that pertains to life and death. To you belongs whatever pertains to men and women.

...

Hail Osiris Khenti-Amentiu! Your mother Nut gave birth to you in Thebes, and you did become a young man. As soon as you did rise on the earth as a child there was a shout of joy, and Ra heard it in his abode in the Land of the North; hearts rejoice at your birth...

You reach Athribis, and you appear in the form of a bull upon his stand in your name Osiris-Uu, while Isis stands before you. She never leaves you...

A Meriotic Queen slaughtering prisoners of war, from a bas-relief at Nagaa. Human sacrifice is often demanded by vampire-gods.

A section of the hieroglyphic text of the Egyptian Book
of the Dead, praising the vampire Osiris.

Plutarch's Moralia

Plutarch (46 A.D. to 120 A.D.) was a Greek biographer and historian. Excerpts are based on a translation by Frank Cole Babbitt.

[Plutarch calls Set 'Typhon']

356.13 One of Osiris's first acts was to deliver the Egyptians from their destitute and brutish manner of living. He taught them agriculture, gave them laws, and religious worship. Later he travelled over the whole earth, educating its people without recourse to arms, through his persuasive discourse, song and music. Thus the Greeks identify him with Dionysus.

...Typhon treacherously plotted against him with seventy-two conspirators... he secretly measured Osiris's body and made a beautiful chest corresponding to its size, which he caused to be brought forth to a party. The company admired the chest, and Typhon promised to present it to the man who found it to be exactly the right length. They all tried in turn, but no one fit. Osiris got into it and lay down. The plotters ran to it and slammed down the lid, nailed it shut and sealed it with molten lead...

363.14   ...Isis wandered everywhere at her wits end; she questioned everyone, even when she met some little children she asked them about the chest. As it happened they had seen it, and they told her the mouth of the river through which the friends of Typhon had launched the coffin into the sea...

358.18   Isis took the coffin to her son Horus, who was being brought up in Buto, and hid the chest away. But Typhon, hunting

Scene from the stone of Narmer, king of the Ist dynasty,
showing the offering of ten decapitated men to Osiris.
Around 3000 B.C.

by moonlight, came upon it. Recognizing the body he divided it into fourteen parts and scattered them, each in a different place. Isis learned of this and searched for them, sailing through the swamps in a papyrus boat...

The only part of Osiris's body which Isis did not find was the penis, because this had been tossed into the river and eaten by fish: the lepidotus, sea-bream, and pike; that is why Egyptians do not eat these species. But Isis made a replica of the member to take its place, and consecrated the phallus in honor of which the Egyptians even today hold a festival.

361.27   ...But the avenger, Isis, the sister and wife of Osiris, after she had quenched and suppressed the madness and fury of Typhon, was not indifferent to the contests and struggles which she had endured, nor to her own wanderings nor to her many deeds of wisdom and feats of bravery, nor would she accept oblivion and silence for them, but she intermingled, in the most holy rites, portrayals and suggestions and presentations of her experiences at that time, and sanctified them, both as a lesson in godliness and an encouragement for men and women who find themselves in the clutch of like calamities.

FURTHER READING

The Book of the Dead, translated by E.A. Wallis Budge

Osiris by E. A. Wallis Budge

Moralia by Plutarch

Diodorus Siculus

Cybele, the Mother of the Gods, personified as the Greek
Demeter, goddess of agriculture and fertility. British
Museum.

CYBELE

Cybele is a doubly enigmatic figure. An incarnation of the Earth Mother, possibly once the female almighty god, she was greatly reduced in stature by the replacement of matriarchal by patriarchal society and religion. Then, like the other deities of the Roman empire, she had her religion, temples, and followers destroyed by Christianity. What we know of her for certain is scant and often guesswork based upon pictures and short inscriptions on archeological remains. She is mentioned with little detail in the surviving Roman writings. Our best sources, though none too good, are early Christian writers; a few of their attacks on her and her followers survive as parts of longer works arguing for Christianity and against paganism.

Her cult is believed to have developed in Phrygia, in Asia Minor (modern Turkey). Its classical center was at Pessinus on Mt. Dindymus; but it was widespread in the ancient world. The Greeks identified Cybele with a variety of female gods, including Rhea, the mother of Zeus. Hera was a sanitized, good-wife version of the Earth Mother, and Demeter, the goddess of agriculture and fertility, acted as another manifestation. The Romans called Cybele Mater Deum Magna Idaea —— Great Idaean Mother of the Gods. In other places she was called Inanna, Ishtar, Anat, Atargatis, Dictynna, Baubo, or Allat. Her cult was established in Rome after her priestesses said Hannibal would be expelled if she were worshipped in Rome; he was and her temple was set up there in 204 B.C.

Was Cybele merely a symbol, or did she have an actual human existence? It is thought that she, and sometimes her followers, were baptized in the blood of a bull, giving them eternal life. She usually had a consort, a young god who died and who she brought back to life: variously called Sumuzi, Tammuz or Adonis. Her annual festival took place from March 15 to the 27th of each year. First a pine tree was cut and brought to her shrine. Then, after days of prayer and fasting, her high priest drew blood from his arm and offered it to her, as did the lower clergy and all her followers. Some went much further, wounding themselves multiple times. This was accompanied by a frenzy of dancing and music, and, in an altered state of consciousness, those men who wished to become her servants castrated themselves.

Bana, a seventh century Indian author, states that the goddess Chandika was worshipped in the Vindhya mountains of Central India by men who wounded themselves to offer blood to her, and even their own flesh. India being no further from Asia Minor than Rome, we can infer that Chandika and Cybele were equivalent. In Hinduism the Great Goddess was worshipped in the shakti cult, in varying aspects such as Parvati, Shiva's bride, and Kali, god of death and demander of human sacrifice.

Doubtless most of Cybele's temples were staffed only by priests and statues, but it is most likely that a real woman or women were behind the cult, which took real blood offerings. When she died, and how long she lived, we do not know.

FURTHER READING

When God Was A Woman by Merlin Stone

The White Goddess by Robert Graves

HOMES OF THE VAMPIRES

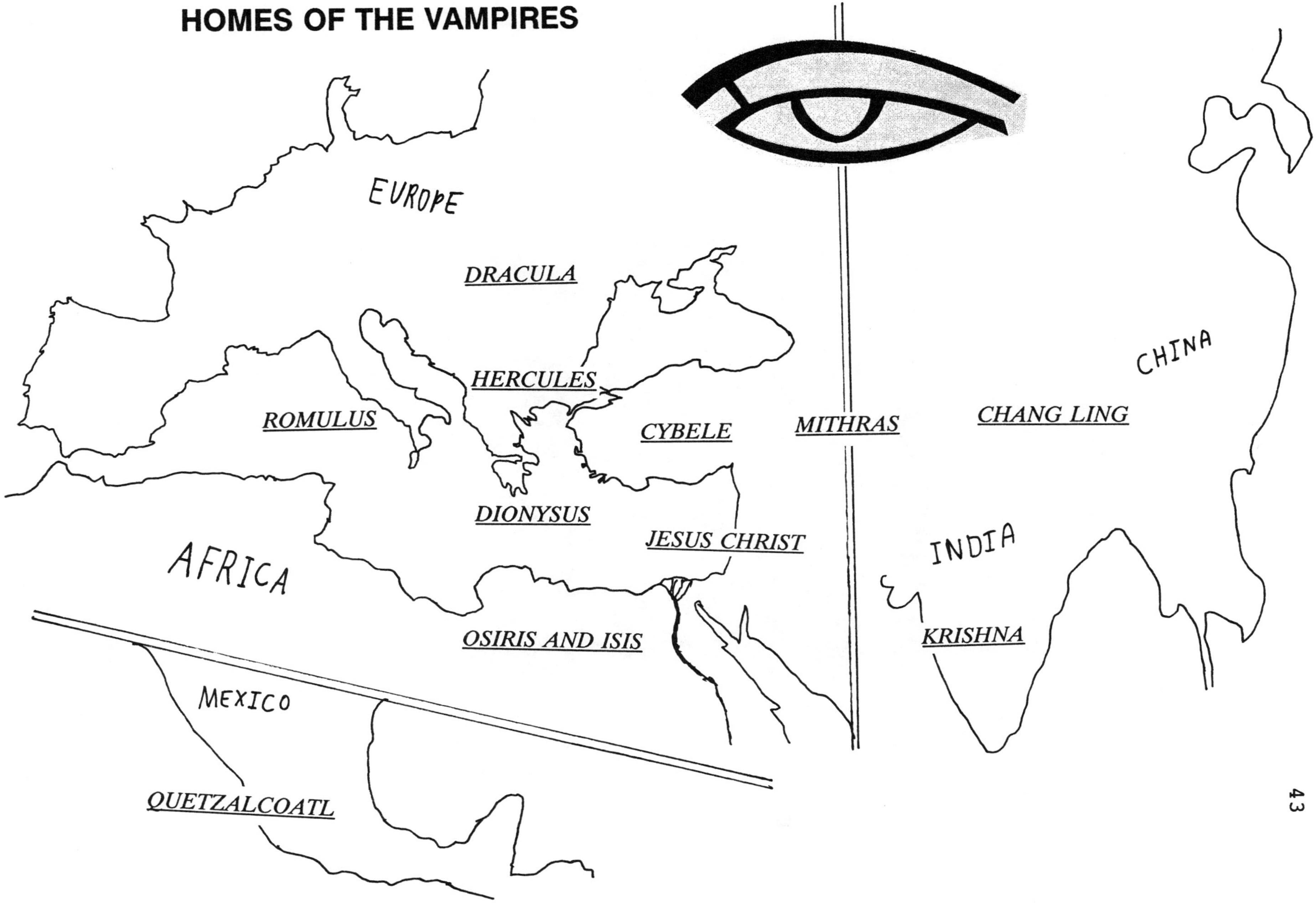

CHINA

CHANG LING

INDIA

KRISHNA

MITHRAS

EUROPE

DRACULA

CYBELE

HERCULES

JESUS CHRIST

DIONYSUS

OSIRIS AND ISIS

ROMULUS

AFRICA

MEXICO

QUETZALCOATL

Cybele riding a Bull, probably representing Mithras,
Osiris or Dionysus.

DOCUMENTS

Crowns of Martyrdom
(Peristephanon Liber)

by Prudentius

Prudentius (4th Century A.D.) was a Christian writer. Excerpts are based on the Prudentius [Loeb Classical Library] translation by H.J. Thomson, D. Litt.

Chapter X

Beginning at Line 196:

Or shall I go to Cybele's pine-grove? No, for in my way stands the lad who castrated himself because of her lust, and by that wound, cutting off his penis, saved himself from the unchaste goddess's embrace, a eunuch for whom the Mother has to lament in many a rite.

Beginning at Line 1059:

There are rites in which you mutilate yourselves and maim your bodies to make an offering of the pain. A worshipper possessed thrusts the knife into his arms and cuts them to propitiate the Mother goddess. Frenzy and wild whirling are thought to be the

Young man about to be initiated into the mysteries of
Cybele, from the city Eleusis. If he is lucky he will
gain immortality, but his lot is probably to give his
life for Cybele's eternal youth.

rule of her mysteries. The hand that spares the cutting is held to be undutiful, and it is the barbarity of the wounds that earns heaven. Another makes the sacrifice of his genitals; appeasing the goddess by mutilating his loins, he unmans himself and offers the shameful eunuch's gift. The source of the man's seed is torn away to give her food and increase through the flow of blood. Both Sexes are displeasing to her holiness, so he keeps a middle gender between the two, ceasing to be a man without becoming a woman. The Mother of the Gods has the happiness of getting herself beardless ministers with a sharp razor! And there is the time when the aspirant to holiness receives the seal; they put little needles in furnaces and then, as soon as they have made them red-hot, burn their bodies with them, and whatever part of the body in branded with the mark of the hot iron they claim to be thus consecrated. Later on, when the man is dead and the spirit has left him and the funeral procession is passing to the tomb, plates are laid along these same parts, a splendid sheet of gold spreads over the skin, and what was burned with fire is covered with metal. Such are the sufferings pagans are compelled to bear, such the law their gods impose on their worshippers; this is how the devil himself makes sport of those whom he has taken captive, teaching them to suffer accursed indignities and ordaining that marks of torture be branded on his luckless victims. But this blood of ours flows from your barbarity; it is you pagans who by your godless cruelty make sores on the bodies of innocent men. If you let us [Christians] alone, we live without shedding blood; but if we are made to suffer bloodshed we win the victory. But now I shall say no more; the appointed end is near, the end of all my ills, the glory of my passion. No longer, you monster, will you be allowed, as you have just been, to rack and cut my flesh; you must needs retire beaten and give up the contest.

48

Mithras slaying a bull, from the underground Temple of
Mithras at Heddernheim. The bull's blood, mixed with
soma, was supposed to confer immortality.

Mithras

The earliest known mention of Mithras dates from the fourteenth century before Christ. Like most other vampire religions, his lasted until about the fourth century A.D., when it was forcibly supplanted by Roman Christianity.

The story of Mithras begins in the area now known as Iran (formerly Persia), but the cult spread fairly rapidly both east to India and west to Asia Minor (Turkey) and eventually to Rome and even Brittain. Mithras (or Mitra or Mithra) played a prominent role both in the the holy scriptures of India, the Vedas, and in the scriptures of ancient Persia, the Avestas. In both he was a god of goodness associated with the Sun and with Justice and contracts. He was also closely associated with the practice of Astrology, and depicted as the god of war and warriors.

Unlike some of the other ancient immortals, there is no clear record of his conversion from an ordinary man to an immortal; he enters history as a god. Moreso than many of the gods, however, he interacted directly with people, rather than representing some remote natural force.

Mithras was a model vampire; one of the greats who most contributed to the modern vampire "myth". True, he did not drink human blood. Rather, he was almost always depicted as slaying a bull, and it was the bull's blood that confered immortality [another legend says it was a mixture of bull fat and soma that was the true elixir]. Very likely the bull was symbolic, though bones of bulls are commonly found when Mithras's temples are excavated. The bull was represented by the constellation Taurus, and also was the symbol of the Egyptian vampire Osiris. Very likely it meant that Mithras either defeated Osiris in battle or that Mithras had drunk Osiris's blood in order to gain immortality.

Worshippers gathering around the dead bull, preparing to
drink its blood, from the underground Temple of Mithras
at Heddernheim.

The cult of Mithras is said to have been extremely secretive, and unfortunately its secrets were lost in the holocaust/inquisition by which early Christians destroyed their rivals. However, many of its temples remain, thanks probably to their secret locations. Almost all were underground; they often were enlargements of natural caves. Thus we have the contradiction that the supposed sun god and his followers abhored the sun and prefered dark crypts for their meetings. The cult, in Roman times, had seven grades, corresponding to the seven known planets (the Sun, Moon, Mercury, Venus, Mars, Jupiter and Saturn). The grades were the Crow, the Hidden One, the Soldier, the Lion, the Persian, the Courser of the Sun, and the top grade, that of Father.

Vows were taken not for a lifetime, but for all eternity. Women were totally excluded from the cult, though apparently many of the male members were married. An important part of the worship of Mithras was a sacred meal including bread, blood, and wine, which Christians claimed was a mockery of Christ's communion. More likely it was a model for it, since it predated it by centuries. At least one depiction of that meal shows crosses inscribed on the bread loaves.

And finally, Mithras always took ground transportation; he was afraid of travel by water.

Mithraism, which both predated and then derived in part from Zoroastrianism, told of a future triumph of good and light over evil and darkness; an Apocalypse. In it Mithras would return to earth and preside over the resurrection of the dead. As with the Christ-cult, exceptional initiates might live to see the return of Mithras, that is, become immortal before the great resurrection.

Mithraism was also closely associated with rule by Kings. The fact that Mithras had divinely chosen a king was supposed to be illustrated by a real halo. Many kings were even named after Mithras, for instance Mithradates Eupator, the most formidable opponent of Rome during the last century of the Republic. The Roman emperors themselves often adopted Mithraism. As early as Nero, eastern kings paying homage declaired that Roman emperors had the favor of Mithras. Lucius Aelius Aurelius Commodus, emperor of Rome from 180 to 192 A.D., is known to have been initiated into the cult. To a large extent the cult of the Emperors as Gods was merged with Mithraism.

Mithraic mass or communion, from Konjica, Bosnia. Note
the crow to the left.

It has often been said that one factor that allowed Christianity to triumph over Mithraism was that the Christ-cult admitted women, whereas the Mithras-cult excluded them. But in fact the Mithras cult came to be closely associated with that of the Earth Mother, or Cybele. In fact their temples were often next door to each other.

Perhaps it is a mere coincidence, since temples of Mithras are found throughout the former Roman empire, but a particularly large contingent are found in modern Rumania. That is to say, in what were formerly known as Wallacia, Moldavia, and Transylvania, the later haunts of Vlad the Impaler, also known as Dracula.

DOCUMENTS

Rig Veda

The Rig Veda is the oldest Indian scripture, written before 1200 B.C. The following excerpts are based on H.H. Wilson's translation.

Second Ashtaka, First Adhyaya, Anuvaka VIII, Sukta II

6   Mithras and Varuna, hear these my invocations, and moreover listen to those uttered everywhere in the chamber of sacrifice; and may Sindhu the renowned bestower of wealth hear us and water our fields.

7   I praise you, Mithras and Varuna, for your gift of numerous cattle and abundant food. Bestow nourishment on me, come quickly, each in your favorite chariot.

Above: Mithras and a Scythian Prince, on a silver cup from Karagodeuashch. Below: four coins with images of Mithras. The one at the lower right is from Tarsus in Asia Minor, where Jesus's apostle Paul grew up.

8   I laud the treasures of the rich; may we, men who are blessed with excellent descendants, partake of them together, the man who confers abundant food has been my benefactor, and has made me the master of horses and chariots.

9   The man who does you wrong, Mithras and Varuna, who injures you in any way, who does not present you with oblations, contracts for himself sickness in his heart. But he who praises you:

10   He, carried by well-trained horses, endowed with surpassing strength, renowned above men, munificent in gifts, moves a hero, ever undaunted in all combats against mighty men.

11   Royal bestowers of delight, listen to the prayer of your undying worshipper, and then come here, that you who traverse the sky may be propitiated by the greatness of the wealth presented to you by the sacrificer, who acknowledges no other protector.

Second Ashtaka, Second Adhyaya, Anuvaka XX, Sukta IV

1   Come, Mitra and Varuna, to our sacrifice, where we press out Soma juice with stones. These juices mixed with milk are exhilarating. Come to us, royal divinities, dwellers in heaven, our protectors; these juices are mixed with milk for you, Mitra and Varuna; they are pure, mixed with milk.

2   Come, for these dripping Soma Juices are mixed with curds; they are pressed out and mixed with curds; whether they be prepared for you at the awaking of the dawn, or associated with the rays of the sun, the juices are effused for Mitra and Varuna, for drinking at the sacrifice.

Second Ashtaka, Second Adhyaya, Anuvaka XXI, Sukta XII

1   Heaven and Earth have been terrified by the strength and noise of him, who pious worshippers, desirous of acquiring cattle, have generated by their sacred acts, amidst the waters of the firmament, at the sacrifice, as a friend for the preservation of living beings, the benefactor of man, and entitled to adoration.

2   Since the priests, like friends, have prepared for you, Mitra and Varuna, a drink of the abundantly flowing and spontaneous Soma juices, therefore do you consent to come to the rite of the worshipper, and listen, showerers of blessing on the household.

3   For the sake of obtaining great strength, showerers of benefits, men glorify your birth from heaven and earth, which is to be extolled, inasmuch as you give the worshipper what he desires as a reward for his sacrifice, and accept the rite that is solemn with praise and oblation.

...

Second Ashtaka, Second Adhyaya, Anuvaka VIII, Sukta XIII

1   Robust Mitra and Varuna, you wear vestments of light. Your natures are without defect. You annihilate all falsehood. You associate with us when we sacrifice.

2   He amongst those of your followers who observes truth, who is considerate, who is commended by the wise, who is able to inflict harm, carefully considers his means. He slays a less-well-armed enemy, and thereby the revilers of the gods, however mighty, shall perish.

3   Who knows, Mitra and Varuna, that it is your doing, that the dawn is the precursor of animals, and that your child the sun sustains the burden of this world. He diffuses the light of truth and disperses the darkness of falsehood.

4   We behold the lover of the maiden dawns [the sun], ever in movement, never resting for an instant, wearing inseparable and diffusive radiance, the beloved abode of Mitra and Varuna.

Second Ashtaka, Second Adhyaya, Anuvaka VIII, Sukta XIV

1   Mighty Mitra and Varuna, dispensers of butter, we worship you, rejoicing, with offerings, with reverent homage, and with oblations of water, so that our priests may propitiate you with our devotions.

[Well, if you are going to be a zombie of a vampire, you might as well get your fair share of butter for it.]

FURTHER READING

The Mysteries of Mithra by Franz Cumont. This is the standard text.

Mithras, the Secret God by M.J. Vermaseren

The Mihir Yast, within the Zend-Avesta

Coin depicting Dionysus. Drachma from Naxos, c. 500 B.C.

DIONYSUS

Whether you consider Dionysus [or Dionysos] to be a god, vampire, or just a myth, he's certain to stir your passions. Even today, sixteen centuries after he and his followers were exterminated by Christians, his name is associated with joy, especially for women.

Dionysus, like Osiris, in many ways is typical of gods who formed the basis for the vampire legend. He is the god of wine, but the wine represents blood. He was torn to pieces and then reborn. He performed acts of magic — miracles. He can appear as a variety of animals, particularly as a snake, goat, or bull. His followers are intoxicated with his presence, zombies — but frenetic rather than sedate ones.

When Dionysus came to Athens in the 7th century B.C. he had long been dead and resurrected. His arrival was an important event, for he became a rival of already well-established gods. The arrival is well recorded both in literature and in vase paintings. He established a cult, with women as priestesses, which quickly grew to be one of the most important in Athens. He and his followers later spread the cult throughout the Greek world and then the Roman Empire. Interestingly in 186 B.C. the cult was banned in Rome by a somewhat puritanical Roman Senate, but for the most part it was tolerated, like all religions, by the Roman Empire.

How old was Dionysus when he arrived in Athens? Very likely he had been alive for at least a millennia. While the historical record is unclear, much evidence points to his origin in Crete, which had one of the most advanced civilizations on earth until about 1100 B.C. There were also persistent rumors

A woman taking delight in the presence of satyrs. Attic
vase, 5th century B.C., Boston Museum.

that Dionysus lived in Egypt prior to living in Crete, but more likely he was added to the Egyptian pantheon after leaving Crete.

Dionysus was totally in control of his cult when he introduced it to Greece, so how much truth was transmitted was up to him. In Crete society had been matriarchal, which is to say that women held the balance of power versus men in society. Female gods were more important than male gods, and the rulers were women, and their daughters in turn. Yet men were not unimportant: they had their role in society and there were male gods.

A very important concept of Cretan culture was the immortality of life, or zoe. One could kill a goat but there would always be goats; disease might take a woman, but there would always be people. Mother Earth was wondrous in her fertility.

By the time of Christ there were several different stories ("myths") current about Dionysus. A common one was that he was both a man and the son of Zeus (but remember, Zeus was a Greek introduction, with no clear parallel in ancient Crete) who played at being an ancient Johnny Appleseed, teaching the culturing of grapes rather than apples. On arriving at the Island of Ikaros he was murdered by the natives, who were suspicious of strangers. A grape vine grew out of his corpse, and later Dionysus (known on that island as Ikaros or Eccaros) reappeared. Probably what happened was that he got up from a death like state and proceeded to plant vines. In any case this story seems to take place a century or three before his arrival in Athens.

Eventually the Greeks invaded Crete and destroyed Cretan civilization, at the same time learning from it, attempting to imitate it, and reviving it. As in other places where a matriarchy was conquered by patriarchal invaders, in Crete male rulers and gods alike acquired legitimacy through marriage to their female counterparts.

In Crete the Great Goddess was the Earth Mother. One aspect of her was the Goddess of the Underworld, responsible both for the dead and for vegetable life that sprang from the ground each spring. Dionysus, the great, anonymous Cretan snake god had a well established cult. In a brilliant political move he declared himself the son of Zeus and Persephone, a Greek goddess equivalent to the Goddess of the Underworld.

Dionysus attended by worshippers, Attic vase, 5th century
B.C., Naples Museum.

Dionysus the Snake God is found in the Jewish Old Testament as Lucifer, the snake who gets Eve pregnant and thus engenders the human race. But Dionysus enjoyed life and hence was no stern, frowning Yahweh, but a generous and good god, a partying kind of God. We also see the snake, or dragon, again in Draco, the Order of the Dragon, and Dracula.

Dionysus's second aspect was the bull. You may be familiar with the story of the Minotaur, the half-man half-bull who ruled the famous labyrinth (maze) of Minos. In Greek times the legend had evolved to this: the Minotaur lived in the labyrinth built by Daedalus and was annually fed 7 young males and 7 young females from Athens, until he was killed by Theseus. But in Crete the labyrinth represented Death and the Underworld. The bull, Dionysus, ruled the underworld. Oddly Ariadne, who was supposed in later legends to give Theseus the thread that allowed him to escape from the labyrinth after killing the Minotaur, was also considered to be the wife of Dionysus.

In fact, in a more mystical treatment of our story, the Snake is father to the Bull, who in turn is father to the Snake. But this Cretan, male, envy of woman's central role in the process of procreation does not seem to be a part of the cult that spread throughout the Mediterranean world after about 700 B.C.

Dionysus's cult was for women, in a society that was highly patriarchal, yet where women had only recently lost their high status. When he arrived in Athens he is said to have married the Queen of Athens. He introduced wine, which helped reintroduce and revive orgiastic rituals. Like Jesus he found it easier to invade the mental space of his followers when they were intoxicated.

There were a number of rituals associated with the worship of Dionysus, some of them public, some private, and some very esoteric. Men were generally allowed only to attend the public rituals, which involved following Dionysus or a representative symbolizing him, and drinking wine. One public ritual all women participated in, one day each year, was swinging (as on a playground-type swing).

Another ritual required the services of one, preferably young, man. It was essentially a dancing, singing and sex orgy for women; its practice was what was prohibited in Rome in 186 B.C., to no avail. At times, out of their minds with ecstasy, the women would tear the representative of Dionysus to pieces.

Hermes holding the infant Dionysus. At his cult's sacrifice a baby goat was killed just after its birth, then boiled in its mother's milk. The kid represents Dionysus, who died and then rose from the dead.

But the truly sacred ritual was a reenactment of the dismemberment and resurrection of Dionysus. Its essence involved slaughtering a baby goat, boiling it in its mother's milk, and feasting upon it. It was this practice that was specifically prohibited to the Hebrews: "Thou shalt not seethe a kid in its mother's milk" Exodus 23:19 and 34:26. Thus the Kosher practice of separating milk products from meat products.

In many places these rituals were practiced on a two year, rather than annual, cycle. This was because Dionysus slept underground for a solid year. The rituals of the women were to re-awaken him, so that he could fill the earth with pleasure and life, until his ritual death, marking the beginning of another year buried in the earth.

DOCUMENTS

The Bacchae

by Euripides

The Bacchae is believed to have been written by Euripides near the end of his life, around 407 B.C., over 300 years after Dionysus arrived in Greece. These excerpts are based on several translations.

Dionysus: I, Zeus's child, now return to the land of the Thebans.
Call me Dionysus, instilled long ago in Semele
By the passionate snaking thunderbolt of love.
I attend this mortal coiled in my human form,
As I come now to Dirce's stream and the water of Ismenus.
Close by the palace I view my mother's monument
The ruins of her home smolder still, the divine fire
Is still alive, Hera's undying insult to dear mama.
All praise Semele's father, Casmus, who keeps

This ground holy, a shrine to his daughter.
But it was I who wreathed it with the vine.

I have come from Lydia's fields, teeming with gold.
I conquered the Persian's sun drenched plains
And the walled towns of Bactria,
Even the wintry land of Media and Arabia.
All Asia is mine, all that lies by the salty sea,
All that possesses towered cities thronged
By Greeks and barbarians both.
This, Thebes, is my first stop in Hellas.
Everywhere else I have instituted my dances and my mysteries
That my eternal light might be manifest to mortals.

First of all Greece are Theban women rejoicing in orgasm.
I have fitted the fawn skin to their bodies and
Have put into their hands the reed entwined with ivy.
For my mother's own sisters, who should have known better,
Said that Dionysus was no son of Zeus.
Said Semele had given her love to some mortal.
Said that, schooled by Cadmus, she blamed on Zeus her own sin.
That is why Zeus killed her, they gossiped,
Because she had lied about her lover.
These same sisters, therefore, I have driven in mad frenzy from
their homes; they live in the mountains, out of their minds.
I have clothed them in my orgies, while the women of Thebes
I drive from their homes to join the mad passion.
Together they sit beneath the trees, on barren rock.
This city must learn to celebrate my Bacchic rites.
My mother's cause I must defend by showing these mortals
The glory of heaven, the Son of Zeus.

Pentheus, Cadmus's grandson, now is king.
He opposes my worship and scorns my name.

A sacrifice to Dionysus, from the bas-relief at the temple of Dionysus in Athens.

Dionysus, a bronze statue depicting him as eternally
young. Found at Pompeii. Naples Museum.

Therefore I will reveal myself to him and to all Thebes
That I am a god. Having triumphed here, on to another land.
Pentheus tries to drive away my Bacchants by force of arms,
So I lead my Maenads into battle against him.
So I have assumed this mortal form,
Appearing as a natural man.

...

Herdsman: Pentheus's mother Agave in frenzy raced past
And I jumped out, assuming to seize her from my ambush.
She raised a cry: "My fleet sisters, we are hunted!
But follow me, wands in hand for weapons!"

We herdsmen fled and escaped their wrath.
They came upon the cows grazing in the pasture
And with bare hands attacked them.
They tore the cows and calves apart.
Limbs of animals were tossed about, dripping blood.
Bulls too were tripped and dragged to the ground
By crowds of young women.
Their flesh was torn asunder faster than the eye blinks.
Like birds the women soared over the ground,
Scouring the spreading plains by the streams of Asopus
Which grows the fine harvests of Thebes.
This invading army fell upon Hysiae and Erythrae,
Nestled on Cithaeron's slopes, swirling chaos,
Pillaging homes at random.
The loot they put upon their shoulders;
Nothing fell to earth, neither brass nor iron.
They carried fire in their curls, yet it burned them not.
Some of us, angered by their depravity, took up arms.
There was a terrible sight to see!
Our pointed spears drew no blood, while

Dionysus partying down with some groupies. If still
living today, he is probably posing as a rock star.
Pottery by the artisan Hieron, found in Etruria. 5th
century B.C.

The women flung their flimsy wands and wounded us
Till we turned and ran. Women defeating men!
There was a god with them. Then they went back
To the fountains of milk and wine the god provided.
They washed off the blood, and serpents licked them clean.

The deity then, whoever he is, my King, receive him
Into our city. He is in many ways powerful.
They say, too that he gave mortals
The wine that ends sorrows. If he exists not
Then neither does Cypris, nor other joy for men.

I am fearful of speaking out freely to one who is my master,
But I say: there is no god greater than Dionysus.

Diodorus Siculus

This compiler and historian lived from approximately 80 B.C. to 20 B.C. While he was even more distantly removed from the events we described than Euripides, he had access to a variety of ancient documents that are no longer available. He repeats almost everything he read and heard, leaving the reader to sort out truth from fiction. The following is only a tiny fragment of his writings on Dionysus.

Re the "Libyan" Dionysus, whom Siculus believed was a predecessor to the Greek Dionysus:

Book III, Chapter 73

Since the Libyans, before the battle, had told Dionysus that at the time when [Dionysus's father] Ammon had been driven from the kingdom, he had prophesied to the inhabitants that at an appointed time his son Dionysus would come, and would recover

Dionysus, shown as Pan, with a woman and angel. 100 B.C.
National Archeological Museum of Athens.

his father's kingdom. After becoming master of all the inhabited world, he would become a God. Thus Dionysus, believing his father to have been a true prophet, established there the oracle of his father, rebuilt the city, and ordained honors to Ammon as a god, as well as appointing priests to have charge of the oracle. Tradition also has recorded that the head of Ammon was shaped like that of a ram...

After Dionysus had built the city and established the oracle he inquired of the god with regard to his expedition, and his father replied that, if Dionysus showed himself a benefactor of mankind, he would become immortal. Consequently elated in spirit at this prophecy, he first directed his campaign against Egypt and as king of the country he set up Zeus, the son of Cronus and Rhea, though he was still a child. As his guardian he named Olympus, by whom Zeus had been instructed and after whom he came to be called Olympian when he had attained pre-eminence. Dionysus taught the Egyptians, it is said, both the cultivation of the grape vine and how to use and store both wine and other fruits gathered from trees. Since a good report of him was spread everywhere, no man opposed him as an enemy. All eagerly obeyed and honored him like a god with praises and sacrifices. In like manner as in Egypt he visited the entire inhabited world, bringing the land under cultivation by means of the plantings which he made and bestowing on the people great and valuable gifts. Thus it is that though different nations are not united in the way they worship most gods, in the case of Dionysus all nations attest to his immortality. There is no man among Greeks or barbarians who does not share in the gift and favor this god dispenses. Even the wilderness tribes learned from him how to cultivate barley and prepare a drink little inferior to wine.

Returning from India, Dionysus learned that the Titans had united their forces and crossed over to Crete to attack Ammon. Zeus had joined with Ammon and war had begun, which Dionysus, Athena and others rushed to join. A great battle raged and

74

Two small bronze representations of Hermes with the infant Dionysus. The Louvre.

Dionysus slew all the Titans. Later, when Ammon and Dionysus became immortal Zeus became king of the entire world, as there were no Titans to oppose him...

Chapter 74

The second Dionysus, who was born to Zeus by Io, the daughter of Inachus, became King of Egypt and created the initiatory rites of that land. The third Dionysus sprung from Zeus and Semele and became, among the Greeks, a rival of the first two. Imitating the principles of his predecessors he led an army over all the inhabited world and left commemorative pillars to mark its bounds. He brought land under cultivation and selected women to be his soldiers, as the older Dionysus had done with the Amazons. He went beyond the others in developing the orgiastic practices, and as regards the rites of initiation, he improved some of them, and introduced others. But since in the long passage of time the former Dionysus's had been forgotten by a majority of men this final Dionysus fell heir to both the plan of life and the fame of his predecessors.

Book IV, Chapter 3

The Boeotians and other Greeks and the Thracians, in memory of the campaign in India, have established sacrifices every other year to Dionysus, and believe that at that time the god reveals himself to human beings. Consequently in many Greek cities every other year Bacchic bands of women gather, and it is lawful for the maidens to carry the thyrsus and to join in the frenzied revelry, crying out "Eiuai" and honoring the god while the matrons, in groups, offer sacrifices to the god and celebrate his mysteries. They sing hymns extolling Dionysus's presence, acting the part of the Maenads who, as history records, were companions of the god from way back...

A rather feminine portrait of Dionysus, bust of marble,
British Museum.

Some story writers, however, relate that there was a second Dionysus who lived much earlier in time than the one just mentioned. According to them there was born of Zeus and Persephone a Dionysus who is called by some Sabazius and whose birth and sacrifices and honors are celebrated at night and in secret because of the disgrace resulting from the intercourse of the sexes. They state also that he excelled in sagacity and was the first to attempt the yoking of oxen and by their aid to effect the sowing of the seed, this being the reason why they also represent him as wearing horns.

And here's a taste of the Greek:

Book IV, Chapter 9:

Της Ακρισιου τοινυν Δαναης και Διος φασι γενεσθαι Περσεα τουτω δε μιγεισαν την Κηφεως Ανδρομεδαν Ηλεκτρυωνα γεννησαι, επειτα τοντω την Πελοπος Ευρυδικην συνοικησασαν Αλκυηνην τεκνωσαι, και ταντη Δια μιγεντα δι απατης Ηρακλεα γεννησαι. την μεν ουν ολην τον γενους ριζαν απ αμφοτερων των γονεων εις τον μεγιστον των θεων αναφερειν λεγεται τον ειρημενον τροπον. την δε γεγενημενην περι αντον αρετην ονκ εν ταις πραξεσι θεωρηθηναι μονον, αλλα και προ της γενεσεως γινωσκεσθαι. τον γαρ Δια μισγομενον Αλκμηνη τριπλασιαν την νυκτα ποιησαι, και τω πληθει τον προς την παιδοποιιαν αναλωθεντος χρονου προσηυηναι την υπερΒολην της τον γεννηθησομενον ρωμης. καθολου δε την ομιλιαν ταυτην ονκ ερωτικης επιθυμιας ενεκα ποιησασθαι, καθαπερ επι των αλλων γυναικων, αλλα το πλεον της παιδοποιιας χαριν. διο και Βουλομενον την επιπλοκην νομιμον ποιησασθαι βιασασθαι μεν μη Βονληθηναι, πεισαι δ ονδαμως ελπιζειν δια την σωφροσυνην την απατην ουν προκριναντα δια ταυτης παπακρονσασθαι την Αλκμηνην, Αμφιτρυωνι κατα παν ομοιωθεντα.

FURTHER READING

Dionysos, Archetypal Image of Indestructible Life by C. Kerenyi, translated from German by Ralph Manheim

Diodorus Siculus

Moralia by Plutarch

Metamorphoses by Ovid

HERCULES

The story of Hercules (here we will use the common English spelling, from the Latin, rather than the Anglicized Greek 'Heracles') is certainly obscured in the dim mist of history. His life as a mortal is supposed to have coincided with early Greek historical figures who may themselves be only dimly based on real people. A possible historical date for Hercules would be around 1200 B.C., coincidental with Theseus's alleged reign as king of Athens. Since Homer is thought to have composed The Iliad in the 8th Century B.C., and Greek history was transmitted for centuries after that by memorization rather than writing, such history must be taken as speculative, like the Jewish mythology.

However speculative Hercules's story is, it certainly fits both the vampire and the mortal-made-god stories, and deserves to be examined here. Hercules was the son of Zeus by the mortal woman Alcmene. However, Zeus's wife Hera was jealous because of his infidelity, and made life for Hercules as difficult as she could. Like Jesus, who was the rightful King of the Jews, Hercules had been intended as the king of the Greeks, but Hera contrived to place Eurystheus on the throne instead. Then she attempted to kill Hercules by sending two serpents to attack the infant; instead he strangled them. Zeus then bargained with Hera, the result being that they agreed that if Hercules completed twelve labors set forth by Eurystheus, he would become immortal and take his place among the gods.

More likely Hercules, clearly a Greek God like Zeus, and a leader of a patriarchal society, engaged in a life and death struggle with the rulers of Crete, who were females heading a matriarchy, and were usually pictured

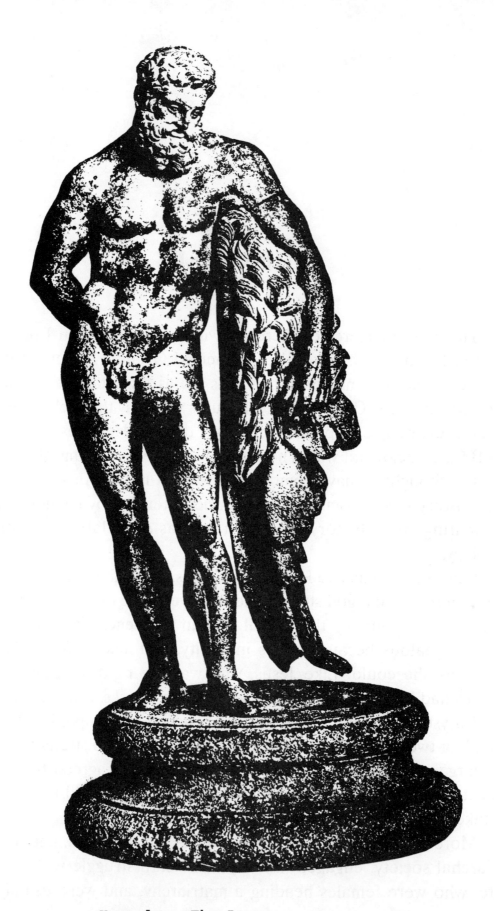

Hercules. The Louvre.

holding a serpent in each arm. Whether he became immortal because of his genetic endowment (Zeus impregnated not only his mother, but several of her ancestors), because he learned the secrets of the Cretan or Egyptian vampires, or for some other reason, history does not record.

There is no point here to repeating the story of Hercules's 12 labors, which consisted mainly of killing mythical and super-strong beasts. It is significant that he descended into Hades and returned alive. Probably this symbolizes his first death and resurrection, after which he walked and continued to be active in war and politics. In fact he not only rose from death himself, but he returned from Hades with Theseus, king of Athens. Later, however, he died, allegedly of poisoning, and ascended into heaven to rule beside Zeus.

While Hercules did not drink blood, he is certainly portrayed as bloodthirsty. He killed not only soldiers in battle, and dangerous beasts, but his own children.

There were many temples to Hercules in the ancient world, including one near Rome that dates back to before the founding of that city, but his cult had little apparent influence on religion, at least not from 600 B.C. onward, for which we have a relatively good written record. His appears to have been a crude religion with little of the psychological appeal to be found in other religions and vampire cults.

Zeus. King of the Greek gods, but not the creator of the universe, he was the alleged father of both Hercules and Dionysus. Did his genes account for their immortality?

DOCUMENTS

Heracles

by Euripides

This play was written around 435 B.C., over 200 years after Dionysus arrived in Athens and probably 800 years after Heracles's birth in the 13th century B.C. Numbers in brackets refer to the first line number of each section.

[1]

Amphitryon: What mortal lives who has not heard my name, Amphitryon of Argos, who shared my wife
with Zeus? I am he: son of Alcaseus
Perseus' son, but father of Heracles.
Here I settled, in this Thebes, where once the earth
was sown with Dragon Teeth and sprouted men.

[606]

Heracles: You advise me well. I will go within.
I owe first greetings to my household gods
because they brought me home from sunless caves
of Kore and Hades. I shall not slight them.

Amphitryon: Did you really descend to Hades, son?

Heracles: Yes; I brought back the triple-headed dog Cerberus.

Amphitryon: You subdued him? Or was he the goddess's gift?

84

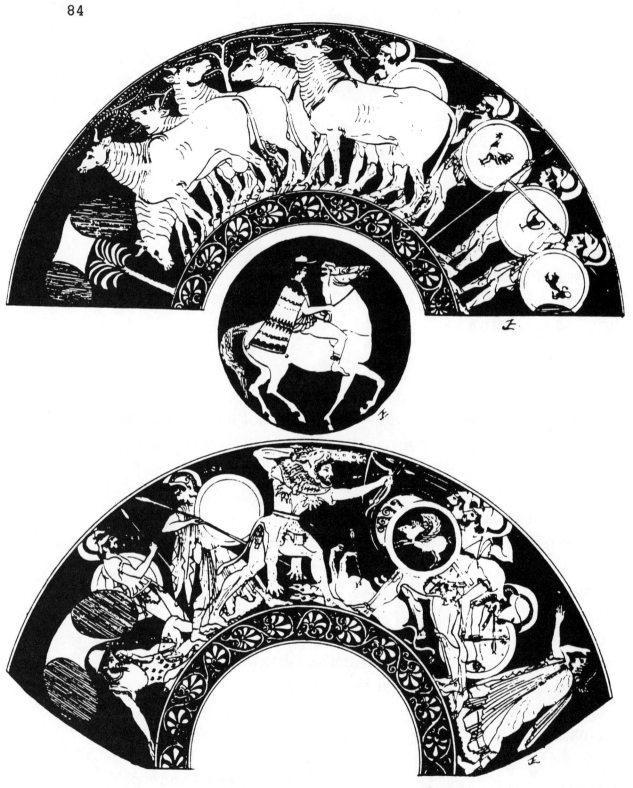

The battle between Hercules and Geryon.   Ceramic cup by
Euphronius, Athens, 5th century B.C.

Heracles: Subdued him. Luck was mine: I saw the mysteries.

Amphitryon: And is the monster at Eurystheus's house?

Heracles: No, at Hermione, in Demeter's grove.

Amphitryon: Does Eurystheus know of your return above?

Heracles: No, I came here first to learn of you.

Amphitryon: Why did you delay so long underground?

Heracles: To save Theseus from Hades, Father.

Amphitryon: Where is he now? Gone to his native land?

Heracles: He went to Athens, rejoicing to be free.

[637]
Chorus: Youth I long for always.
But old age lies on my head,
a weight more heavy than Aetna's rocks;
darkness hides the light of my eyes.
Had I the wealth of an Asian king,
Or a palace crammed with gold,
both would I give for youth,
Loveliest in wealth,
Loveliest in poverty.
But old age I loathe: ugly, murderous.
Let the waves take it
So it comes no more to the homes and cities of men!
Let the wind whirl it away forever!

A 5th century B.C. vase found at Apulia. Representing
Hades, it shows, among others, Hercules's wife and sons,
slain by the god in his madness, on the left; Hercules
himself has seized the dog Cerberus to prove that he has
descended into hell and returned alive.

[797]

Chorus: The marriage bed two bridegrooms shared!
One was man, the other, Zeus
Who entered in the bridal bed
and with Alcmene lay.
How true, O Zeus, that marriage proves to be!
Your part in it, against all doubt, is proven true!
For time at last has clearly shown the strength
Of Heracles the hero.
He made his way from Pluto's halls;
He left the dungeon underground.

[821]

Iris: Courage, old men. You see there, Madness,
Child of night, and myself, Iris, servant of the gods.
We bring no harm upon your city;
Against one man alone our war is waged:
Heracles, whom men call Alcmene's son by Zeus.
Until his bitter labors had been done,
His fate preserved him; nor would father Zeus
Let me or Hera do him any harm.
But now Eurystheus' orders have been done,
Hera plans, by making him destroy his sons,
To taint him with fresh murder, and I agree.
Up then, unmarried child of blackest night,
Rouse up, harden that relentless heart,
Send madness on this man, confound his mind
And make him kill his sons. Madden his feet:
Drive him, goad him, shake out the sails of death
And Speed his passage over Acheron,
Where he must take his crown of lovely sons.
Let him learn what Hera's anger is,
and what is mine. For the gods are nothing,
And men prevail, if this one man escapes death!

[1279]

Heracles: And now my last worst labor has been done:
I slew my children and crowned my house with grief.
And this is how I stand: I cannot stay
With those I love at Thebes. If I remain
What temple, what assembly of friends will have me?
My curse is unapproachable.
Go to Argos then? No, I am banished there.
Settle in some other city, then,
Where notoriety torments me,
Watched and goaded by bitter taunts?
"Is this the son of Zeus, who killed his wife and sons?
Away with him. Let him die elsewhere."

Theseus: No other god is implicated here, except Hera,
The wife of Zeus. Rightly you judge.
My advice is this: be patient, suffer
What you must, and do not yield to grief.
Fate exempts no man; all men are flawed,
As are the gods, unless the bards do lie.
Do not the gods commit adultery?
Have they not cast their fathers into chains
In pursuit of power? Yet all the same
Despite their crimes, they live upon Olympus.
How dare you then, mortal that you are,
To protest your fate, when the gods do not?

Diodorus Siculus

This compiler and historian lived from approximately 80 B.C. to 20 B.C. While he was even more distantly removed from the events we described than Euripides, he had access to a variety of ancient documents that were consequently lost. He repeats almost everything he read, leaving the reader to sort out truth from fiction. The following is only a tiny fragment of his writings on Hercules:

Book IV, Chapter 8

I am aware that difficulties beset those who try to give an account of the ancient stories, and that this is especially true of the myths of Hercules. Regarding the greatness of his deeds, it is generally agreed that Hercules has been remembered as a man who surpassed all men we know of, from the beginning of time. Therefor it is difficult to report each one of his deeds in a worthy manner; the very magnitude of his deeds being such that he won immortality... We shall relate his deeds from the beginning, basing our account on the most ancient poets and writers.

9. God lay with Acrisius, and begot Danae. He lay with Danae and begot Perseus, who married Eurydice, and thus begot Alcmene, who was in turn loved by Zeus and bore Hercules. Consequently he descends on both sides from the greatest of the gods. This divine component was seen not only later in his deeds, but was recognized even before his birth. For when God lay with Alcmene he made the night three times its normal length and expended that time on procreation, presaging the coming might of his child. He did not effect this union from the desire for love, as he had with other women, but only for the sake of procreation. Consequently he did not take Alcmene violently, nor could he

Hercules with a stag, 4th Century A.D., just before his
cult was exterminated by the Christians.

hope to persuade so chaste a woman; instead he impersonated her husband, Amphitryon.

When the natural time of pregnancy had passed God announced in advance in the presence of all the gods that it was his intention to make the child born that day king over the descendants of Perseus. Then Hera, filled with jealousy, with the aid of her daughter Eileithyia, stopped the birth pains of Alcmene and brought Eurystheus to birth before his time. God, though he had been outgeneralled, wished to keep his promise and ensure the future fame of Hercules. He persuaded Hera to agree that Eurystheus should be king, but that Hercules should serve Eurystheus and perform twelve labors, as prescribed by Eurystheus, and that after doing so Hercules would be made immortal...

10.   After this Hera sent two serpents to destroy the babe, but the child, instead of being terrified, gripped the neck of a serpent in each hand and strangled them both...

14.   A peculiar thing also came to pass in connection with Hercules's birth. The first mortal woman raped by Zeus was Niobe, the daughter of Foroneus, and the last was Alcmene, who was the sixteenth lineal descendent from Niobe. Thus Zeus began to beget human beings with the ancestors of this Alcmene and ceased with her; that is, he stopped with her his intercourse with mortal women, as he had no hope to beget one worthy of his former children...

16.   ...The commander of the Amazons, Melanippe, who was also greatly admired for her courage, he then slew. Heracles, having thus killed the most renowned Amazonians and forced the rest to flee, cut down the greater number of them, so that their race was utterly exterminated...

He gathered his army on Crete, having decided to make his departure from that place. The island was especially well situated

Hercules wrestling the giant Antaius. This was just one of the many feats which caused Zeus to reward Hercules with immortality. Hercules's great strength is often attributed to vampires.

for expeditions against the far reaches of the world. Before his departure he was magnificently honored by the natives, and wishing to show his gratitude to the Cretans he cleansed the island of the wild beasts which infested it. And this is why in later times not a single wild animal, not bear, nor wolf, nor serpent, was to be found on the island...

21.   ...it would come to pass that any man making a vow to tithe to Hercules would lead a happy and prosperous life. And in fact this custom did arise and persists still. Many Romans, even men of great wealth, who have taken a vow to dedicate a tithe to Hercules had thereafter become happy and prosperous...

26.   Heracles, then, according to the ancient stories, descended into the realm of Hades. Welcomed like a brother by Persephone, he freed Theseus and Peirithous and brought them back to the upper world. He received from Persephone the dog Cerberus in chains, and carried him away to the amazement of men...

31.   Apollo answered him: Hercules would be rid of his disease if he sold himself as a slave and honorably paid over the purchase price to the sons of Iphitus [whom he had unjustly killed]. Being constrained to obey the oracle, he sailed to Asia with some friends. There he willingly submitted to be sold by one of his friends and became the slave of Omphale, the daughter of Iardanus, who was still unmarried and was queen of the people who were called at that time Maeonieans, but now Lydians...

After this Hippocoon exiled from Sparta his brother Tyndareus, and the sons of Hippocoon, twenty in number, put to death Oeonus who was the son of Licymnius and a friend of Heracles; whereupon Heracles was angered and set out against them, and slaughtering them all was victorious. Taking Sparta by storm he restored Tyndareus, who was the father of the Dioscori, to his kingdom and bestowed upon him the kingdom by right of

Hercules depicted on a Macedonian coin from 330 B.C.
Alexander the Great (356 to 323 B.C.) of Macedonia was a
worshipper of Hercules. He conquered nations as far away
as India, where he found the priests already knew of
Hercules and Dionysus, confirming histories saying they
too ventured that far.

war, commanding him to keep it safe for Hercules own descendants...

38.   Hercules, having abandoned hope for himself, ascended the pyre and asked each one who came up to him to set it afire. When no one had the courage to obey him, Philoctetes was prevailed upon. Having received in return the bow and arrows of Hercules, he lit the pyre. Immediately lightning also fell from the heavens and the pyre was wholly consumed. When the companions of Iolaus came to gather up the bones of Hercules and found them not, they knew that, in accord with the oracle, he had passed from among men into the company of gods.

FURTHER READING

Moralia by Plutarch

The Greek Myths by Robert Graves

Shield of Heracles by Hesiod

Idyll by Theocritus

Heracles; Children of Heracles by Euripides

Pausanias

Trachinian Women by Sophocles

Metamorphoses by Ovid

Krishna with snake, bronze statue, 15th Century A.D.,
Tamilnadu, India. Asian Art Museum, San Francisco.

Krishna

The story of Krishna as presently told is many layered. Even with all the whitewashing of the last 2000 years he is today a clearly vampire-like deity.

Krishna does not appear in the Vedas, the literature of the Aryan conquerors of India probably written between 1500 and 1200 B.C. Because he first appears in the Upanishads, written between 600 and 300 B.C., and because he is dark (Krishna means black) like the pre-Aryan population, we can safely conclude that he was a non-Aryan vampire whose cult was gradually incorporated into the Brahmanic mainstream of Hinduism. We can also conclude that stories of the teenage and baby Krishna written in relatively recent times serve only as propaganda or imaginative literature. In addition many popular elements of the Cults of Dionysus and Christianity were added, with no apparent purpose except to attract a maximum number of people into Krishna's own cult. While the worship of Krishna is not as popular as the worship of Jesus, still it must be counted as one of the more successful vampire-cults of modern times.

The story given in the Bhagavad Gita (Song of the Blessed One, a portion of the Mahabharata, written circa 200 B.C.), as supplemented by the Puranas, is that Krishna was an incarnation of Vishnu, a supreme benevolent deity. His uncle was King Kamsa of Mathura, who ordered a slaughter of the innocents because it was foretold that Krishna would slay him. Krishna is a prince, son of King Vasudeva of Dwarka. Arjuna, a central figure, marries Krishna's sister Subhadra. Then, because of injustices committed, Krishna urges Arjuna to war against his usurping relatives. Krishna gives Arjuna advice during the battle, mainly urging him to slay his relatives, saying their souls are

Krishna playing a flute. Originally a bloodthirsty
warrior-king, like Osiris his priests did a media
relations campaign over the centuries to make him more
Dionysian. Stone statue, 15th Century A.D., Asian Art
Museum, San Francisco.

Krishna, close up of the statue from opposing page.

immortal so killing them isn't unethical. Arjuna's side wins the battle and eventually Krishna kills Kamsa and rules over Mathura. Later Krishna dies when a hunter accidentally shoots him in the foot with an arrow. However, since he is really a god he resurrects himself at will.

Thus we have the typical story of a deified warrior king, not unlike Osiris, Hercules, and Quetzalcoatl. However, the Bhagavad Gita has a more important purpose than recording Krishna's supposed life. Salvation, it claims, is to be obtained by devotion to Krishna. Eternal life can be yours if you give up your mortal life and obey Krishna or his current cult leaders. Hey, why think when someone else is willing to do your thinking for you?

But after the Bhagavad Gita, in which Krishna appears to be totally bloodthirsty, his cult added quite a few elements to try to make Krishna acceptable and hence popular. He became a flute player and a sex god, a sort of Indian Dionysus. He also performs a number of miracles to prove his divinity. Like Hercules he kills beings sent to destroy him even when he is a baby, and like Jesus he is to be accepted as a personal savior, saving people the trouble of dealing with avoidance of sin and punishment (karma).

DOCUMENTS

Bhagavad Gita

Believed to have been written around 200 B.C.; based on various translations.

Chapter 18

55   Man comes to know me [Krishna] truly through love. Worshipping me, aware of my greatness, he enters straight into me. Even the man who must work, if he leans on me, reaches Nirvana by my grace.

Vishnu, the second member of the Hindu trinity and called
"The Preserver." Krishna was his most important human
incarnation. Statue from 12th Century A.D., Bangladesh.
Asian Art Museum, San Francisco.

Give me your heart, let me be your Master. Do not try to think or reason, but give your mind to me.

Absorbed in me, we will fly over difficult ground. But alone you will perish. You cannot refuse to kill your brothers, as I command. Son of Kunti, your murderous nature will prevail.

Arjuna, Lord of all beings, hides in their hearts; through him they spin on the wheel of life and death.

Abide in him alone, with all your being, son of Bharata. Through his grace you will achieve peace in eternity.

Thus have I revealed the great secrets. Consider them, then act as you will. Listen again to my highest, most secret words. I love my own wisdom, and tell you for your own good.

Fix your mind on me, be my slave, worship me, kowtow before me. Come to me alone. My promises are true: you are dear to me.

Forget tradition and ethics. Let me be your sole shelter. Do not be sad, I will deliver you from all evil.

Don't repeat what I have said to men who are not disciplined and slavish or who will not listen uncritically or who are prone to argue.

But he who transmits my secrets to my devotees, who himself loves me alone, he will surely become part of me. No man on earth could please me more.

FURTHER READING:

The Child Krishna, Christianity, and the Guyars by J. Kennedy in the Royal Asiatic Society Journal, 1907, p. 951

The Puranas

Durga or Parvati, an Indian vampire goddess and relative
of Krishna. Statue from the 11th century A.D., Asian Art
Museum, San Francisco.

Quirinus with the Earth Mother.

ROMULUS OR QUIRINUS

What was the secret of the success of the Roman Empire? How did a mean village in the days of mighty Athens and Persia and Carthage come to be a vast and long-lived empire, existing in one form — the Roman Catholic Church — even today?

The Romans attributed much of their success to their gods, especially their almighty Trinity: Jupiter, Mars, and Quirinus. You have doubtless heard of Jupiter, the all-powerful equivalent of the Greek god Zeus, and of Mars, the war god. But who was Quirinus? A minor deity, eclipsed over time by more popular ones?

No, Quirinus was popular enough among the Romans. He was unpopular with Christians, however, because he was a rival to Christ — perhaps a living rival. Like Dionysus, Osiris, Mithras and Hercules, he died beneath the Christian sword, and was subsumed into the Christian pantheon of holidays, rituals, and saints. Even in The United States of America, a nation founded by deists, agnostics and atheists, Quirinus's history has been a closely guarded secret, for fear of Christian retaliation.

Rome was founded by Romulus and Remus. The king of Alba, Amulius, had seized the thrown from his brother Numitor and murdered members of his family to insure his rule. He named his niece, Rhea Silvia, a vestal virgin, to prevent her from having offspring who might rival his own. Rhea was raped — she claimed by Mars — and her twin sons were condemned to die at birth of exposure. However, [like Krishna, Jesus, Moses, and Hercules] they escaped that fate. A she-wolf suckled them until they were found by Faustulus, the king's herdsman, who raised them as his sons. Thus, like Jesus, though

TIME LINE OF
THE ROMAN EMPIRE

770 B.C.	Romulus and Remus born
753 B.C.	Rome founded by Romulus
715 B.C.	Romulus ascends into heaven
509 B.C.	King expelled; Republic founded
347 B.C.	Gauls capture, but are then expelled from, Rome
266 B.C.	All Italy conquered by Rome
27 B.C.	Augustus becomes first Emperor All Mediterranean held by Empire
4 B.C.	Birth of Jesus Christ
12 A.D.	Gaius Caesar (Caligula) born
27 A.D.	Jesus crucified and resurrected
37 A.D.	Caligula Emperor
41 A.D.	Caligula assassinated
100 A.D.	Reign of Trajan The Empire's greatest extent
306 A.D.	Constantine becomes first Christian Emperor
379 A.D.	Theodosius Emperor; persecutes non-christians
395 A.D.	Empire divided: Western and Eastern Empires
410 A.D.	Goths seize Italy Roman Catholic Church replaces Western Empire
1453 A.D.	Turks complete conquest of Eastern Empire

descended from Kings they are raised as commoners, and stand in opposition to the powerful.

After heroically restoring Numitor to the thrown of Alba, Romulus and Remus founded their own town. Romulus killed Remus and became the sole ruler of Rome. By his skill as a statesman and warrior he protected the town and caused it to prosper. In the end he disappeared from his thrown in the midst of a violent storm. His divinity was immediately proclaimed by his soldiers. The next day Romulus appeared to senator Julius Proculus, saying: "Go and tell my people that the gods, from whom I came, will that Rome shall be a great city and capital of the world. Let them practice self restraint and valor. Let them know, and teach to their children, that no power on earth shall stand against Roman arms. Now I go to dwell in heaven, as the gods will." Then Romulus rose bodily into the heavens. This occurred about 715 B.C.

And indeed Romulus's prophecy became true, albeit slowly at first. Was Romulus immortal, or a vampire, and did he guide Rome's development into the world's greatest empire?

If Romulus lived on earth after his observed ascent into heaven his existence was clothed in secrecy. Officially he was identified with Quirinus, a pre-existing deity. The whole situation is quite odd by any analysis. If Romulus was the earthly double of the heavenly Quirinus, then there is no need for him to be the son of Mars. If, like Hercules, he was the son of a god who by his merits was admitted into heaven, then why identify him with Quirinus? If he was merely a deified king, as cynics would have it, why identify him with Quirinus, and why not extend his deeds, by fable, until long after his death? And why is Romulus, a warrior and son of Mars, identified with Quirinus, who was a god of agriculture and peace?

It took a long time for Rome to become an even minor power in the ancient world. It took a hundred years to incorporate the Latins in the immediate surrounding area. A bit more of Italy was annexed in the next two centuries, covering the time of the greatest extent of the Persian Empire. The Gauls entered Rome and burnt it in 390 B.C. Then suddenly, between 300 and 200 B.C., all of Italy was conquered. Between 200 B.C. and 100 B.C. Rome conquered Greece, defeated Carthage, and annexed Spain and Numidia. By the time Christ was born Rome ruled the entire Mediterranean world. Yet in the histories that survived the Christian era book-burnings, Romulus and Quirinus do not appear to have intervened to help Rome, in war.

Quirinus, however, did have a priesthood. According to Livy the Trinity each had an official priesthood created by Romulus's elected successor, King Numa. Numa also appointed the first Pontiff, or Pope, Numa Marcius. Numa's reign was marked by peace and by the adoption of high ethical standards by Rome's citizenry.

Several historians have tried to piece together the scant clues we have about the nature of Quirinus, and hence Romulus. Here we look at the clues from a different angle: was Romulus immortal, was he a god or vampire, and did his legend contribute to the vampire "myth?"

Quirinus was associated with lesser deities, several of whom were associated with specific actions related to the harvesting and storing of grain. The Romans were, at least during the period of the republic, vegetarians whose staple was grain. Perhaps, then, Quirinus is related to Dionysus and Osiris, both of whom were alleged to have introduced agriculture in the ancient world. Romulus was, like Hercules and Osiris, a conqueror, but his conquests were minor by comparison.

Quirinus's name is thought to be derived from curia, which designated the smallest divisions of the primitive Roman tribes. Quiritis meant, in fact, Roman citizen. The fact that Romulus founded Rome, and is identified with Quirinus, attests to Quirinus being the genuine god of the Romans as a people or organization of people. This was reflected in offerings of war spoils: Jupiter's were taken from the king or consul's booty, Mars from the professional officers, and Quirinus's from the common soldiers. In return his greatest gift was to watch over the all important supply of grain, including its fair distribution among the common people. Originally Quirinus may even have been a goddess of fertility or earth mother, or her husband/counterpart, as was Dionysus. Perhaps this relates to another mystery, Quirinus's priests' participation in the rites of the mysterious Larentia, who was a quasi-deity of fabulous wealth who secretly supported the Roman people.

Perhaps Romulus, founder of the greatest of the empires, was the greatest of the gods, or the smartest of the vampires. For now these mysteries remain unsolved.

DOCUMENTS

From The Founding of the City

by Livy

Livy lived from 59 B.C. to 17 A.D. He began this history around 26 B.C. This excerpt is based on B.O. Foster's translation, 1919.

Tiberinus was succeeded by Agrippa, Agrippa by his son Romulus Silvius, who was struck by lightning and bequeathed his power to Aventinus. Aventinus was buried on the hill, now a part of the city of Rome, and gave the hill his name. Proca, the next king, had two sons, Numitor and Amulius. To the elder, Numitor, was bequeathed the ancient realm of the Silvian family. Yet violence proved more potent than a father's wishes or respect for seniority. Amulius drove out his brother and seized the throne. One act of violence led to another; Amulius proceeded to murder his brother's male children, and made his own niece, Rhea Silvia, a Vestal virgin, ostensibly to her honor, but actually to deprive her of the hope of children.

But the Fates were resolved, I suppose, that this great city of ours would arise, and the first steps would be taken towards the founding of the mightiest empire the world has known, outside of heaven. The Vestal Virgin was raped and gave birth to twin boys. Mars, she declared, was their father, perhaps believing that, perhaps hoping to thereby decrease her guilt. But neither gods nor men protected her or the babies from the king. The mother was bound and flung into prison; the boy's, by the king's order, were condemned to be drowned in the river.

Destiny, however, intervened. The Tiber had overflowed its banks; because of the flooded ground it was impossible to get to the actual river, and the men entrusted to do the deed thought

Mars, the alleged father of Romulus, and part of the Roman trinity with Jupiter and Quirinus.

that the flood-water, sluggish though it was, would serve their purpose. Accordingly they carried out the king's orders by leaving the babies on the edge of the first flood waters they came to. At that spot now stands the Ruminal fig tree, said to have once been known as the fig tree of Romulus. In those days the country there was wild and uncultivated, and the story goes that when the basket in which the infants had been exposed was left high and dry by the receding water, a female wolf, coming down from the neighboring hills to quench her thirst, heard the children crying and made her way to where they were. She offered them her teats to suck with such gentleness that Faustulus, the king's herdsman, found her licking them with her tongue. Faustulus took them to his hut and gave them to his wife Larentia to nurse. Some think that the origin of this story was the fact that Larentia was free with her favors and was called Wolf by the shepherds, giving rise to the wolf story.

...

Romulus did not assemble his band of youths, for he was not strong enough for open hostilities against Amulius. Instead he instructed a number of his men to meet at the king's house by different routes at a pre-ordained time. This was done, and with the help of Remus at the head of another body of men, the king was surprised and killed...

After the control of Alba had passed to Numitor, he gave Romulus and Remus permission to found a new settlement on the spot where they had been left to drown as infants. There was already an excess of population at Alba, between the Albans themselves, the Latins, and the brothers' shepherds; enough to hope that Alba and Lavinium would one day be small compared with the proposed new settlement. But the brothers' plan for the future was marred by the same curse which had divided their grandfather and Amulius: jealousy and ambition. A disgraceful quarrel arose... There is another story, a commoner one, according to which Remus, by way of jeering at his brother, jumped over the half-built walls of the new settlement, whereupon Romulus killed him in a fit of rage, adding the threat, "So perish whoever shall leap over my battlements."

This was how Romulus obtained the sole power. The newly built city was called by its founder's name.

Romulus's first act was to fortify the Palatine hill, the scene of his own upbringing. He offered sacrifice to the gods, using the Alban forms except in the case of Hercules, where he followed the Greek ritual as instituted by Evander. According to the old tale, Hercules after killing Geryone came into these parts driving his oxen. The oxen were exceedingly beautiful, and, close to the Tiber, at the spot where he had swum across with them, he came to a grassy meadow. Weary from walking, he lay down to rest and allowed the beasts to refresh themselves in the rich pasturage.

...

On the occasion of which I am writing Evander could not but observe the shepherds who were excitedly mobbing the unknown killer. He joined them, and upon being informed of the crime and its cause, directed his gaze upon the stranger. Seeing him to be of more than human stature and of preternatural dignity of bearing, he asked him who he was, and hearing his name and parentage and country, cried: 'Hercules, son of Jupiter, I bid you welcome. You are the subject of my mother's prophecy, for she, a true prophet, declared: that you would increase the number of the Gods, that here an altar would be dedicated to you, and the nation destined to be the mightiest in the world would one day name it Greatest of Altars and serve it with your own proper rites.'

... This was the only foreign religious rite adopted by Romulus. By doing so he showed his respect for that immortality that is the prize of valor. His own destiny was leading him to the same reward.

Having performed with proper ceremony his religious duties, he summoned his subjects and gave them laws, without which the creation of a unified body politic would not have been possible. In his view the rabble over whom he ruled could be induced to

113

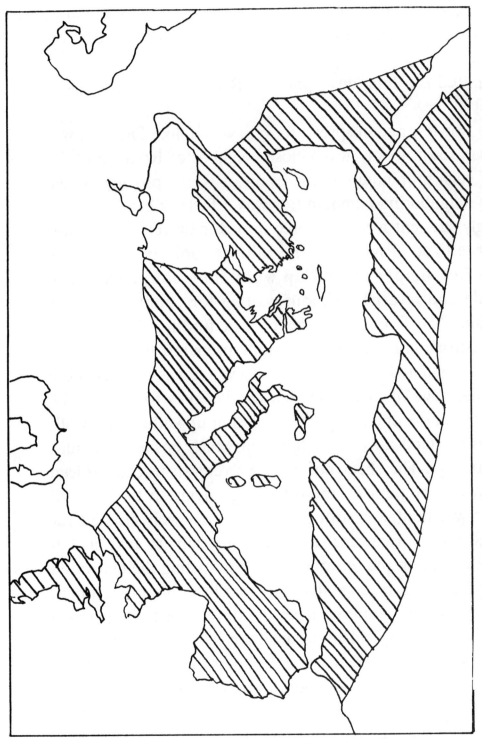

The Roman Empire at its greatest extent, around 100 A.D. The vampire/god cults of Mithras, Cybele, Hercules, Dionysus, Isis and possibly others co-existed within the empire; but the new, intolerant Christ-cult would exterminate them all within 300 years, and in exterminating knowledge and learning, cause the collapse of the empire by 410 A.D.

respect the law only if her himself adopted certain visible signs of power. He proceeded, therefore, to increase the dignity and impressiveness of his position by various devices, of which the most important was the creation of the twelve lictors to attend his person...

[Omitted is a long description of Rome's early wars under Romulus.]

The war fever soon spread to Veii, which, like Fidenae, was an Etruscan town. It was also a close neighbor of Rome, and the danger of such propinquity in the event of Rome proving hostile to all her neighboring communities was a further exacerbation. Accordingly she sent a raiding force into Roman territory. It was not an organized movement; the raiders took up no regular position, but simply picked up what they could from the countryside and returned without waiting for countermeasures from Rome. The Romans, however, not finding them still in Roman territory, crossed the Tiber fully prepared for a decisive struggle, and assumed a position with a view to an assault upon the town. At the news of their approach the Veientes took the field, to fight it out in the open rather than be shut up within their walls and forced to stand a siege. In the fight which ensued Romulus used no strategy. The sheer power of his veteran troops sufficed for victory, and he pursued the retreating enemy to the walls of Veii. The town itself was strongly fortified and well situated for defence. Romulus, accordingly, made no attempt to take it, but contented himself on the return march with wasting the cultivated land, more by way of revenge than for what he could take from it. The loss the Veientes suffered from the devastation did as much as their defeat in the field to secure their submission; they sent envoys to Rome to plead for peace. They lost a part of their territory and were granted a hundred years' truce.

Such is the story of Rome's military and political achievements during the reign of Romulus. All of them harmonize well enough with the belief in his divine birth and the divinity ascribed to him after his death. One need but recall the vigor he displayed in recovering his ancestral throne, the wisdom in founding Rome, and his bringing her to strength by the arts of both war and peace. It was to him and no one else that Rome owed the power which enabled her to enjoy untroubled tranquillity for the next forty years.

Great though Romulus was, he was better loved by the commons than by the senate, and best of all by the army. He maintained, in peace as well as in war, a personal armed guard of three hundred men, whom he called The Swift.

Such were the deeds of Romulus, which will never grow old. One day while he reviewed his troops on the Campus Martius near the marsh of Capra, a storm burst with violent thunder. A cloud enveloped him, so thick that it hid him from the eyes of everyone present; and from that moment he was never seen again upon earth.

The troops, who had been alarmed by the sudden storm, soon recovered when it passed over and the sun came out again. Then they saw that the throne was empty, and ready though they were to believe the senators, who had been standing at the king's side and now declared that he had been carried up on high by a whirlwind, they still felt like children having lost a father, and for a long time stood in sorrowful silence. Then a few voices began to proclaim Romulus's divinity; the cry was taken up, and at last every man present hailed him as a god and the son of a god, and prayed to him to be forever gracious and protect his children. However, even on this great occasion there were a few dissidents who maintained that the king had been torn to pieces by the senators. Anyway, this story got about, in veiled terms, but it was not important, for awe and admiration for Romulus's greatness set the seal upon the other version of his death.

Julius Proculus was a man, we are told, honored for his honesty and wisdom. Proculus addressed the Assembly. 'Romulus,' he declared, 'the father of our City, descended from heaven at

Romulus

dawn this morning and appeared to me. In awe I stood before him, praying for permission to look at his face, without sin. "Go," he said, "and tell my people that the gods, from whom I came, will that Rome shall be a great city and capital of the world. Let them practice self restraint and valor. Let them know, and teach to their children, that no power on earth shall stand against Roman arms. Now I go to dwell in heaven, as the gods will."

Metamorphoses

by Ovid

The poet Ovid (Publius Ovidius Naso) lived from 43 B.C. to 17 A.D. These excerpts are based on the translation by Frank Justus Miller.

Book XIV

Now the Ausonian water-nymphs held a spot near Janus' temple where a cold spring bubbled forth. Venus asked aid of these, nor did the nymphs refuse the goddess her just request, but opened up their fountain's streaming veins. Up to that time the pass of Janus was still open, nor had the water ever blocked the way. Now they placed yellow sulphur beneath their living spring and heated the hollow veins with burning pitch. By these and other means reeking steam filled the fountain through and through, and the waters, which had been ice cold, were as hot as fire itself! The two gate-posts smoked with hot fumes, and the gate, which had been opened to the hardy Sabines, was blocked by the new fountains, so that the Romans could arm themselves. Then

Romulus took the offensive, and soon the Roman plain was strewn with the Sabine dead and with Roman blood as well, the impious swords mingling the blood of son in law with the blood of father in law. At last it was their will to end the war, rather than fight to the bitter end; and it was agreed that Tatius should share the throne.

Tatius had since died and Romulus was meting equal laws to both the tribes when Mars put off his gleaming helmet and thus addressed the father of gods and men: "The time is come, father, since the Roman state stands on strong foundations and no longer hangs on one man's strength alone, to grant the reward which was promised to me and to thy worthy grandson, to take him from earth and set him in the heavens. You said to me, before the council of immortals: 'One shall there be who will be raised up to the azure blue of heaven.' Now let the full meaning of your words be ratified."

The omnipotent god indicated his assent, filling the sky with dark clouds and showering the earth with thunder and lightning. Gradivus knew this for the assured sign of the translation which had been promised him. Leaning on his spear, he mounted his chariot pulled by the steeds in bloody yoke and snapped his whip. Gliding downward through the air, he hovered on the summit of the Palatine Hill. There, as Ilia's son Romulus was giving kindly judgement to his citizens, he caught him up from earth. His mortal part dissolved into thin air, as a leaden bullet hurled by a broad sling is apt to melt away in the mid-heavens. Now a fairer form clothed him, worthier of the high couches of the gods, such as has Quirinus, clad in the sacred robe.

His wife Hersilia was mourning him as lost when regal Juno bade Iris go down to her with these words: "Oh lady, bright glory of both Latium and of the Sabine race, most worthy once to have been the consort of so great a man, and now of divine Quirinus, cease your laments and, if you would indeed behold your husband,

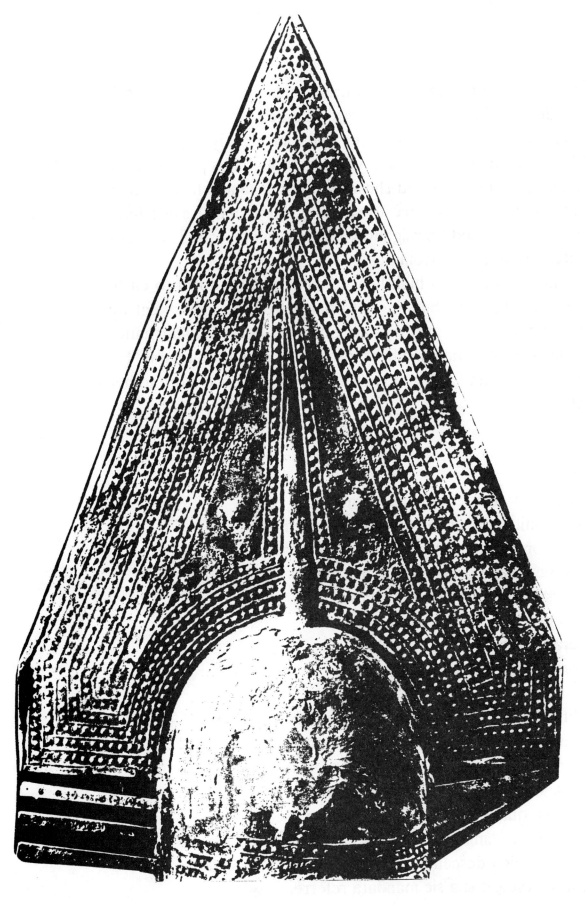

Helmet from the 7th century B.C., Rome, as would have been worn by Romulus and his soldiers in battle.

come with me to yonder grove which stands green on Quirinus's hill, shading the temple of the king of Rome."

Hersilia, scarce lifting her eyes, modestly replied: "O Goddess (for I do not know who you are, though it is plain you are a goddess), lead me on and show me my husband's face. If only the fates grant me but once to see him, then shall I say I have gained heaven indeed." Straightway she went along with Thaumas's daughter to the hill of Romulus.

There a star from high heaven came gliding down to earth and Hersilia, her hair bursting into flame from its light, went up together with the star into thin air. She with dear, familiar hands Romulus received, changing her mortal body and mortal name. He called her Hora, and as a goddess she was joined once more to her Quirinus.

In Latin:

adnuit omnipotens et nubibus aera caecis
occuluit tonitruque et fulgure terruit orbem.
quae sibi promissae sensit rata signa rapinae,
innixusque hastae pressos temone cruento
inpavidus conscendit equos Gradivus
et itu verberis increpuit pronusque
per aera lapsus constitit in summo
nermorosi colle Palati reddentemque
suo non regia iura Quiriti
abstulit Iliaden: corpus mortale per auras
dilapsum tenues, ceu lata plumbea funda
missa solet medio glans intabescere caelo;
pulchara subit facies et pulvinaribus altis
dignior, est qualis trabeati forma Quirini.
Flebat ut amissum coniunx, cum regia Iuno
Irin ad Hersilien descendere limite curvo
imperat et vacuae sua sic mandata referre:

"o et de Latia, o et de gente Sabina
praccipuum, matrona, decus, dignissima tanti
ante fuisse viri coniunx, nunc esse Quirini,
siste tuos fletus, et, si tibi cura videndi
coniugis est, duce me lucum pete, colle Quirini
qui viret et templum Romani regis obumbrat;"
paret et in terram pictos delapsa per arcus,
Hersilien iussis compellat vocibus Iris;
illa verecundo vix tollens lumina vultu
"o dea (namque mihi nec, quae sis, dicere promptum est,
et liquet esse deain) duc, o duc" inquit "et offer
coniugis ora mihi, quae si modo posse videre
fata semel dederint, caelum accepisse fatebor!"
nec mora, Romuleos cum virgine Thaumantea
ingreditur colles: ibi sidus ab aethere labsum
decidit in terras; a cuius lumine flagrans
Hersilie crinis cum sidere cessit in auras:
hane manibus notis Romanae conditor urbis
excipis et prieum pariter cum corpore nomen
mutat Horamque vocat, quae nunc dea iuncta Quirino est.

FURTHER READING

Archaic Roman Religion by Dumezil

Cicero

Lives of the Romans by Plutarch

Caligula as a child. A grandson of Augustus Caesar, as a child he allegedly poisoned his father Germanicus.

GAIUS CAESAR
A.K.A. CALIGULA

Gaius Caesar, better known as Caligula, is included here not so much because there is evidence that he became immortal, as because his life was so similar to better known vampires, especially Dracula.

Caligula is believed to have been born in 12 A.D., towards the end of the reign of Augustus Caesar. His father Germanicus was a general who had married Agrippina, the daughter of Julia, the daughter of Augustus. Thus Augustus Caesar was his great-grandfather. It is important to recall that Augustus was treated as a god in some oriental cities in his lifetime, and was deified by the Roman Senate after his death.

Despite the fact that he was a Roman emperor in a time of great learning, today the information we have on Caligula is both scant and suspect. In Caligula's case we can only partly blame this on Christian book-burning or the general loss of historical records during the "dark ages." His reign was controversial and his enemies were not content to celebrate his death. For reasons unknown the chapters of the annals of Tacitus (c. 115 A.D.) covering Caligula's reign did not survive, though the chapters immediately preceding and following did. Even Tacitus must have based his history on earlier accounts, since Gaius Caesar died in 41 A.D, before Tacitus was born. The best account we have, therefor, is that of Seutonius, writing around 121 A.D.

There is a rumor that Caligula, while a young child, poisoned his father Germanicus, being coached by Gnaeus Piso; very likely a fiction. He was born in a military camp, loved by the soldiers, and received his nickname Caligula,

124

Bust of Nero Caesar, Grandson of Germanicus, Nephew of
Caligula, and first Roman emperor to outlaw Christianity.

meaning Little Boot, from them. Germanicus was also loved by the soldiers and was doubtless poisoned because he was both a popular candidate for Emperor and wanted, instead, to restore the Republic.

In fact it is likely that Caligula was a quite pious child, interested in religion, augury, and mysticism. He was also interested in the arts, theater and dancing. His first, and possibly only, office before becoming Emperor, was that of Pontiff, meaning he would have been in charge of the Roman religious rights of Jupiter, Mars, and Quirinus. Since it was common knowledge that Dionysus, Hercules, Romulus and other mortal men had become immortal gods, it is not surprising that he may have aspired to the same.

The Emperor Tiberius, who had apparently become obsessed with eroticism in his old age, took a liking to Caligula and made him heir to the empire. According to Seutonius, Tiberius appeared to have died and Caligula was declared emperor; when Tiberius arose from his death bed Caligula strangled him.

The former Pope, finding himself Emperor at the age of 25 in 37 A.D., began his reign auspiciously. He inherited the popularity of his father, and was seen as a reprieve from the cruelty of Tiberius. He confirmed this by offering a general pardon, even including people who had conspired to prevent him from becoming emperor. He ended censorship and even had the empire's bookkeeping made a matter of public record.

Then, however, he declared that he was a god and began making bizarre directives. His reign quickly turned bloody, with rich people most at risk: he had them tried and killed on various pretexts, and then added their wealth to his treasury. He forced the noblest Roman women to prostitute themselves to raise money for the treasury, and was known to enjoy watching his victims slowly killed. He claimed to talk to the other Roman gods, established his own religious cult, and, like Osiris and the Egyptian pharaohs, openly had sexual intercourse with his sisters.

Apparently he was a prolific writer, master orator, and competent actor, yet none of his works survived. After his death he appeared as a ghost who haunted his burial grounds; but then he disappeared from history.

As a vampire he doesn't rate well. He was bloodthirsty enough, and weird enough, and as Roman Emperor may have had access to older vampires

Portrait of the family of Augustus Caesar, including
Caligula as a child.

or their wisdom. However, if the story told by Suetonius is true, he can hardly have survived physical death. "As Gaius looked around his jawbone was split with a sword blow. He lay upon the ground, writhing, and called out that he still lived. The others dispatched him with thirty wounds, for the general signal was 'Strike again.' Some even thrust their swords through his privates." His cult probably disbanded on its own, its obsequious members ready to find a way to suck up to the new Caesar, Claudius.

DOCUMENTS

Lives of the Caesars

by Suetonius

C. Suetonius Tranquillus, A.D. 75-140 Translated by John C. Rolfe, 1913, based on Maximilin Ihm's translation of 1907.

IV. 4

With the same degree of popularity he [Caligula] recalled those who had been condemned to banishment; took no cognizance of any charges that remained untried from an earlier time; had all documents relating to the cases of his mother and brothers [who were murdered at Tiberius Caesar's command] carried to the Forum and burned, to give no informer or witness occasion for further fear, having first loudly called the gods to witness that he had neither read nor touched any of them. He refused a note which was offered him regarding his own safety, maintaining that he had done nothing to make anyone hate him, and that he had no ear for informers.

XVI. He banished from the city the sexual perverts called spintriae, barely persuaded not to drown them in the sea. The writings of Titus Labienus, Cremutius Cordus, and Cassius Severus, which had been suppressed by decrees of the senate, he allowed to be hunted up, circulated, and read, saying that it was wholly to his interest that everything which happened by handed down to posterity. He published the accounts of the empire, which had regularly been made public by Augustus, a practice discontinued by Tiberius. He allowed the magistrates unrestricted jurisdiction, without appeal to himself. He revised the lists of the Roman knights strictly and scrupulously, yet with due moderation, publicly taking their horses from those guilty of any wicked or scandalous act, but merely omitting to read the names of men convicted of lesser offenses. To lighten the labor of the jurors, he added a fifth division to the previous four. He also tried to restore the suffrage to the people by reviving the custom of elections. He at once paid faithfully and without dispute the legacies named in the will of Tiberius, though this had been set aside, as well as in that of Julia Augusta, which Tiberius had suppressed. He remitted the tax of a two-hundredth on auction sales in Italy; made good to many their losses from fires; and whenever he restored kings to their thrones, he allowed them all the arrears of their taxes and their revenue for the meantime.

XXII.   So much for Caligula as emperor; we must now tell of his career as a monster.

After he had assumed various surnames (for he was called "Pious," "Child of the Camp," "Father of the Armies," and "Greatest and Best of Caesars"), chancing to overhear some kings who had come to Rome to pay their respects to him, disputing at dinner about the nobility of their descent, he cried: "Let there be one Lord, one King." And he came near assuming a crown at once and changing the semblance of the principality into the form of a monarchy. But on being reminded that he had risen above the elevation both of princes and kings, he began from that time on to lay claim to divine majesty; for after giving orders that such statues of the gods as were especially famous for their sanctity or their artistic merit, including that of Jupiter of Olympia, should be brought from Greece, in order to remove their heads and put his own in their place, he built out a part of the Palace as far as the Forum, and making the temple of Castor and Pollux its vestibule, he often took his place between the divine brethren, and exhibited himself there to be worshipped by those who presented themselves; and some hailed him as Jupiter Latiaris. He also set up a special temple to his own godhead, with priests and with victims of the choicest kind. In this temple was a life-sized statue of the emperor in gold, which was dressed each day in such clothing as he wore himself. The richest citizens used all their influence to secure the priesthood of his cult and bid high for the honor. The sacrifices were of Flamingoes, peacocks, black grouse, guinea-hens and pheasants, offered a single species per day. At night he used constantly to invite the full and radiant moon to his embraces and his bed, while in the daytime he would talk confidentially with Jupiter Capitolinus, now whispering and then in turn putting his ear to the mouth of the god, now in louder and even angry language. He was heard to make the threat: "Lift me up, or I'll lift thee." But finally won by entreaties, as he reported, and even invited to live with the god, he built a bridge over the temple of the Deified Augustus, and thus joined his palace to the Capitol. Presently, to be nearer yet, he laid the foundations of a new house in the court of the Capitol.

XXIV.   He lived in habitual incest with all his sisters, and at a large banquet he placed each of them in turn below him, while his wife reclined above. Of these he is believed to have violated Drusila when he was still a minor, and even to have been caught lying with her by his grandmother Antonia, at whose house they were brought up in company. Afterwards, when she was the wife of Lucius Cassius Longinus, an ex-consul, he took her from him and openly treated her as his lawful wife; and when ill, he made

The Roman Colosseum, where conquered soldiers fought as gladiators. It was built by the Emperors Vespasian and Titus, 75 to 79 A.D. It's predecessor was the site of Caligula's death.

her heir to his property and thrown. When she died, he appointed a season of public mourning, during which it was a capital offence to laugh, bathe, or dine in company with one's parents, wife or children.

LIX. He lived twenty-nine years and ruled three years, ten months and eight days. His body was conveyed secretly to the gardens of the Lamian family, where it was partly consumed on a hastily erected pyre and buried beneath a light covering of turf. Later his sisters, on return from exile, dug it up, cremated it, and consigned it to the tomb. Before this was done, it is well known that the caretakers of the gardens were disturbed by ghosts, and that in the house where he was laid not a night passed without some fearsome apparition, until at last the house itself was destroyed by fire. With him died his wife Caesonia, stabbed with a sword by a centurion, while his daughter's brains were dashed out against a wall.

An Illustration of the Latin text:

LIX. Vixit annis viginti novem, imperavit triennio et decem mensibus diebusque octo. Cadaver eius clam in hortos Lamianos asportatum et tumultuario roto semiambusutm levi caespite obrutum est, postea per sorores ab exsilio reversas erutum et crematum sepultumque. Satis constat, prius quam id fieret, hortorum custodes umbris inquietatos; in ea quoque domo, in qua occubuerit, nullam noctem sine aliquo terrore transactam, donec ipsa domus incendio consumpta sit. Perit una et uxor Caesonia gladio a centurione confossa et filia parieti inlisa.

FURTHER READING

Lives of the Caesars by Suetonius

Jewish Antiquities by Josephus

The Emperor Gaius by J.P.V.D. Balsdon

Quetzalcoatl

Far from the Mediterranean, in the Central Valley of Mexico, at a time when the immortal rivals of Jesus Christ were losing their battle to retain control of the Roman Empire, a man we call Quetzalcoatl created a religious, commercial and political empire that was to last, in one form or another, until the Christian conquest of Mexico in 1521. And, bizarrely, the Spanish Christ-cultists were able to conquer Mexico in part because the Aztecs mistook them for Quetzalcoatl and his followers returning from exile.

As with many of the other vampire-gods, the stories preserved about Quetzalcoatl vary considerably in content. Most of the written record was destroyed in book burning frenzies, the most final of which was organized by the Grand Inquisitor of Mexico, Juan de Zumarraga, in 1535. Add to this conflicting interpretations of the archeological record.

In legends Quetzalcoatl is closely connected to the sacred city of Tollan, which is most likely the very real (and still quite impressive) city of Teotihuacan. According to archeologists this city flourished from about the time of the birth of Jesus until about 700 A.D. However, a smaller city called Tollan, near Mexico City, was founded by a man calling himself Quetzalcoatl in 980 A.D. Quetzalcoatl's mother is usually described as a woman named Chimalma, though sometimes his mother was transfigured into a goddess such as Coatlicue, the earth mother deity. In any case his father died long before he was born. A magical gem that his mother swallowed caused her to become pregnant without a male partner, and his mother died in childbirth, leaving him an orphan. He was a spiritually oriented youth, given to penance and fasting, but also excelling in the arts of war. When his reputation had grown sufficiently

Quetzalcoatl

he was asked by the people of Tollan to become their ruler. He built new temples, taught them new rituals, and expanded trade. Above all, he brought Tollan into parallel with the cosmic city, thus giving it a stability that most cities lacked.

He finally built a special temple, went into deep fast and penance, and ascended through the layers of heaven to the Creative Pair from which all things spring. He learned that he was the human counterpart of the great god Quetzalcoatl, god of wind, and supreme being. Thus, like Jesus and others, he claimed to be the essential link between humanity and God, the active double of the inactive but all-encompassing creator. Following this Tollan became the greatest city of all. Its crafts and farming prospered. Like Findhorn its fruits and squashes were giant varieties of the ordinary vegetables. Cotton grew in abundance and in many colors, so that it could be woven into bright garments without dyes.

In one story, however, due to the chaos of the new age brought forth by his spiritual powers, all of humanity died and had to be revived. Quetzalcoatl descended to the underworld to bring back men's bones, but was tricked by the underworld's demons and died himself. Luckily Quetzalcoatl, the all powerful cosmic god, caused the human Quetzalcoatl to be revived. He then brought forth the bones and caused the people of Tollan to be resurrected.

The cosmos of the ancient Mexicans was marked by great instability. Bringing stability required that the forces of destruction be appeased. Quetzalcoatl did this by introducing human sacrifice, and in particular the heart sacrifice in which still-beating hearts were torn from the chests of victims. The ceremonies certainly involved drinking human blood and eating human flesh. There is no indication that drinking blood made Quetzalcoatl immortal, and his priests who drank the blood were certainly mortal.

Physically, Quetzalcoatl the man had a beard, just like Jesus and Dionysus, but more notable because the native peoples of Mexico were and still are generally beardless. Symbolically the god Quetzalcoatl is represented as a feathered serpent, and the man is usually depicted as wearing a serpent mask.

But, aside from his death and resurrection, Quetzalcoatl has a tragic side. Around 700 A.D. a rival, Tezcatlipoca, appeared. He was a sorcerer who

136

Great Pyramid at Teotihuacan, Mexico; built under the
direction of Quetzalcoatl

Cortes torturing the Aztec emperor Guatemotzin. Some Aztecs thought Cortes was Quetzalcoatl; perhaps he was. The Spanish/Christian conquest of the Americas in the 1500's elevated Christianity from a minor religion to the most important one in the world.

demanded a return to human sacrifice (Quetzalcoatl, his domain now in harmony with the cosmos, had declared that only quail, butterflies, and snakes would be sacrificed). Tezcatlipoca snuck a mirror into the sacred temple and caused Quetzalcoatl to look into it and be horrified: "the eyelids were greatly swollen, the eye sockets deeply sunk, the face much distended all over and bilious." The Tezcatlipoca convinces Quetzalcoatl to become drunk, and when drunk to make love to his "sister."

Realizing that his actions had broken his sacred vows, Quetzalcoatl decided to take his most devoted followers with him to erect a new city-temple. Tezcatlipoca and his faction could destroy, but not govern: Tollan's population quickly dwindled, leaving only the majestic pyramids that still stand today. Quetzalcoatl and his followers conquered the Yucatan, and reigned there several hundred years. Then for reasons unknown he set out upon the ocean in a ship, promising to return at a later, crucial date, the year of One Reed.

Queerly, some Christians have speculated that Quetzalcoatl was Jesus or perhaps one of the apostles. The similarities are rather striking, and the timing could not be better: if Jesus did indeed rise from the dead around 40 A.D., and then leave his followers for another realm, he would have arrived in Mexico in time to be Quetzalcoatl in Teotihuacan. If he left Mexico anytime after 300 A.D., he could have returned to rule over a Christian Roman Empire. If he returned with — or as — Cortes in 1521, he would only be reclaiming what was rightfully his. Interestingly, Cortes showed up in the year One Reed as Quetzalcoatl had foretold. And of course, the slaughter of the Indians by the Spaniards made the Aztec practice of heart-sacrifice seem relatively civilized. The Americas had the souls — and gold — the Catholic Church needed to increase its power to the point where it could become the world's dominant religion, instead of third fiddle to Islam and Buddhism.

FURTHER READING

Quetzalcoatl and the Irony of Empire by David Carrasco
Ancient Mexican Art by Ferdinand Anton
The Conquest of New Spain by Bernal Diaz del Castillo

Mexican hieroglyphics, Teotihuacan. Despite the
Christian Inquisition's effort to destroy the records of
Mexican vampires, some survived; they are subject to much
interpretation.

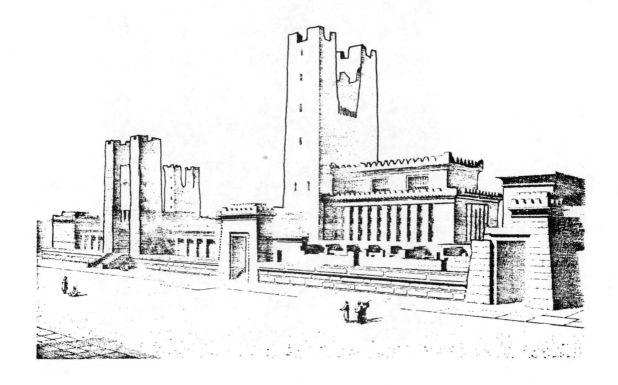

The Temple in Jerusalem as it would have appeared during Jesus's lifetime.

Jesus Christ

In all probability Jesus Christ, worshipped as God by Christians, is the actual secondary model, after Vlad the Impaler, for the modern literary vampire. As many scholars have pointed out, *Dracula* is largely a parody of Christ and Christianity. It was written at a time when many intellectuals thought Christianity, which they saw as wholesale superstition, would collapse under its own weight.

Those readers with even a slight knowledge of Christianity probably have recognized strong parallels between the religions of Mithras, Hercules, Osiris, Dionysus and Christ. But unlike these other religions, Christianity is still going strong. Perhaps the reason is that, as a system of faith, it is better constructed than its regional predecessors. But the case can also be made that these other cults were ruled by vampires who were already quite aged when Christ appeared. Mithras, Hercules, Osiris and Dionysus were all at least 1500 years old by the time Jesus is said to have been born. Romulus, it is true, was some 700 years old when Jesus was born, but his interest lay in a government empire, not a religious cult. In fact the incorporation of Christianity into the system of Roman government by Constantine the Great in 313 AD, an institution still living today as the Roman Catholic Church, may mark the alliance of two vampires rather than the supplanting of one by the other.

Judaism before (and after) Christ recognized one God, Yahweh or Jehovah. Nowhere in the Old Testament is it stated that Yahweh has a son. The promised Messiah was depicted as a liberator, king, or prophet, not as a god. The idea that Jesus was the Son of God, true or not, was Greek or Egyptian, not Hebrew. Just as Hercules and Dionysus were sons of the

Jesus Crucified

Almighty Zeus, Jesus was depicted as the son of Almighty Yahweh. Like Hercules, Dionysus and Osiris, Jesus began as a mortal: his immortality had to be earned in life.

In life, as depicted in the gospels (which of course, could have been propaganda with little relation to reality), Jesus is not a warrior like Hercules, nor a practical farmer like Dionysus. He is a pundit, a lawyer, and a philosopher. He sways people with his mouth and the occasional miracle. In his role as a lawgiver he does reflect both Mithras and Osiris.

His relation to Dionysus he makes clear: "I am the true vine." The drinking of blood and eating of flesh at the last supper, symbolic or not, became the core of the mystic Christian ritual. The Romans, Greeks, and Jews all accused the early Christians of kidnapping babies and sacrificing them, a blasphemous version of the Dionysian sacrifice of a new-born goat. And Passover, the occasion of the Last Supper, was a good holiday to appropriate for the new Christian religion. What was Passover? The Jews say it is the day that the Angel of Death passed over the houses of the Jews, who had marked their doors with blood, and slaughtered the firstborn children of all the Egyptians (Exodus 12). But what really happened, certainly, was gangs of Jews went our at night and engaged in the slaughter, a crime they later sanctified and attributed to their god.

The stress on obedience in early Christianity, as seen in the Epistles of Paul, may have merely been a result of the typical cult leader's need for power. But in vampire mythology the Master is able to control his followers, zombies, by hypnosis or direct will. And in modern Christianity the appearance of Jesus to pentecostalists is followed by a blind obedience and unbending faith. Christians who have been touched directly by Jesus appear to be totally incapable of reasoning: their idea of an argument is to repeat dogma over and over, relentlessly.

The core of Christian belief is that Jesus rose from the dead, and that his followers will do the same. This is also the core of the vampire myth. The myth or reality was elaborately built upon by early Christians. Before his death Jesus was supposed to have revived Lazarus. The Apostle Paul was also said, in the Acts of the Apostles, to have been stoned to death and resurrected. In converting the people of the Roman Empire the Christians claimed, frequently,

Diocletian, Roman emperor from 245 to 313 A.D., tried to strengthen the Roman emperor-god cult and enacted severe laws to defend citizens against the Christ-cult.

that their priests had healed the sick and resurrected the dead. Cynics among the Greeks and Romans, it is true, pointed out that these resurrections were always in the past, and could never be proven by a current example. But for non-Christians to simply dismiss the possibility of the resurrection of Jesus is more dangerous than accepting the possibility while still denying Jesus's divinity. Whether or not Jesus is undead, the Christian religion still is.

Why was Christianity able to overcome older, more established religions as well as the more rational systems of thought that the Greeks had introduced? First, the Roman Empire in its final stage had only just come into existence when Christianity emerged. This made travel throughout the Mediterranean area far easier than had been the case in the past. The other cults, thousands of years old, were mainly content with their existing status, and did not seek to destroy rivals or become universal religions. The Roman government encouraged freedom of religion, only occasionally being forced to outlaw religions that were a clear danger to the social order. The only cult that seriously contended with Christianity after the 3rd century A.D., Mithraism, limited its followership severely: anyone could become a Christian, but Mithraism was open only to an elite. Finally, the Empire needed a new religion of subservience in order to govern easily; Christianity filled that bill. But all these factors together are not as important as the mental construct that Christianity was able to create for its believers.

Christianity is not the simple result of vampire worship. It is a cleverly constructed faith that incorporates elements from Judaism, Dionysus, Mithras, and Osiris. From Judaism it gains it intolerance of other religions. From the cult of Isis and Osiris it took the prerogative of both resurrecting and judging the dead, based on a moral code by which it attempted to control the living. From the cult of Dionysus it took the concept of pitying a suffering god. And from Mithraism it took the concept of converts as warriors who would make their God triumphant even as they triumphed with his aid over their enemies. The Christian was told to think that he was just while pagans were evil, that his reward would be life in heaven instead of death or hell, that he and his fellow Christians were an elect who would triumph on earth, and that his god Jesus had to suffer because of the sins of the pagans. Could any doctrine produce a

Constantine the Great, the first Christian Roman Emperor,
born in 280 and died 337 A.D. He decided disputes among
the many factions of Christians, and called the first
Ecumenical Council in 325 A.D. at Nice, Bythnia, which
adopted a standard creed for the Christian Church.

people more self-righteous, more easily manipulated by their leaders, or more willing to murder innocent people and while declaring themselves saints?

What about the alleged persecution of Christians by the Roman empire? In fact there was little persecution, and generally it was a reaction with the intent to protect pagans from the intolerant, blood-thirsty Christians. Far more Christians perished in sectarian conflicts within Christianity than were killed by the Roman government in the centuries leading up to the establishment of the Christian Church as the official church of Rome. The holocaust that followed, as Christians burned pagan temples, preferably with pagans inside, is matched in history only by the later medieval attempts by Catholics to exterminate the Jews, Albigensians, and Moslems.

Wallachia, later home to Vlad the Impaler, a.k.a. Dracula, was part of the Roman empire and a few days march from Greece, a short hop by boat from Palestine. It was home to many of Mithras's temples. Perhaps the vampire "myth" developed here because of a clearer pagan understanding of Christ and Christianity. Pagan beliefs flourished in Wallachia and neighboring Transylvania at least through the time that Catholicism was introduced by Dracula's father Dracul.

Why do early Christian writings make little reference to a living Christ? We don't know, but there has been much speculation. For the first few centuries of his existence Jesus had powerful rivals; perhaps remaining in hiding was necessary for survival. The apostles and their converts were expendable. Doubtless he did appear to the leaders of his church. To this day the Pope claims to talk to God over lunch; perhaps this is literally true.

148

Theodoseus, 346-395 A.D., consolidated Christianity as
the sole religion of the Roman Empire. He ordered all
other temples destroyed, as well as statues of other
gods, confiscated the property of non-Christians, ordered
them to be tortured and murdered, burned most books, and
instituted the original Inquisition. As a result the
Empire fell apart almost immediately, and never recovered
in learning or industry.

DOCUMENTS

We have only one non-Christian mention of Jesus Christ or Christianity from the century of Christ's life, surprising when one considers the miracles and size of his following that are attributed to him. In fact the Jews in particular liked to record the deeds and words of their holy men, but failed to notice either Jesus or John the Baptist. However, Flavius Josephus wrote volumes on Jewish History and in particular on the Roman-Jewish war of 70 A.D. (which he participated in) yet only one paragraph of his writings concerns Jesus or Christians. It may have been inserted by later Christians, or altered to fit their views. In fact Origen, writing in 280 A.D. specifically states that Josephus did not believe Jesus was the Christ or Messiah. Yet in 324 A.D. Eusebius's version did have the following passage:

Jewish Antiquities

by Josephus

Chapter XVIII, third paragraph

About this time there lived Jesus, a wise man, if indeed one ought to call him a man. For he was one who wrought surprising feats and was a teacher of such people as accept the truth gladly. He won over many Jews and many of the Greeks. He was the Messiah. When Pilate, upon hearing him accused by men of the highest standing among us, had condemned him to be crucified, those who had in the first place come to love him did not give up their affection for him. On the third day he appeared to them restored to life, for the prophets of God had prophesied these and countless other marvelous things about him. And the tribe of Christians, so called after him, has still to this day not disappeared.

In the original Greek:

Γινεται δε κατα τουτον τον χρονον Ιησους σοφος ανηρ, ειγε ανδρα αυτον λεγειν χρη. ην γαρ παραδοξων εργων ποιητης, διδασκαλος ανθρωπων των ηδονη ταληθη δεχομενων, και πολλους μεν Ιουδαιους, πολλους δε και του Ελληνικου επηγαγετο. ο χριστος ουτος ην. και αυτον ενδειξει των πρωτων ανδρων παρ ημιν σταυρω επιτετιμηκοτος Πιλατου ουκ επαυσαντο οι το πρωτον αγαπησαντες εφανη γαρ αυτοις τριτην εχων ημεπαν παλιν ζων των θειων προφητων ταυτα τε και αλλα μυρια περι αυτου θαυμασια ειρηκοτων. εις ετι τε νυν των Χριστιανων απο τουδε ωνομασμενον ουκ επελιπε το φυλον.

The Holy Bible

Excerpts based on the King James version, rendered to modern English by the editor

Gospel of Matthew

Chapter 26

26   And as they were eating, Jesus took bread, and blessed it, and broke it, and gave it to the disciples, and said, take, eat; this is my body.

The Triumphal return from the sacking of Jerusalem, at
the Arch of Titus in Rome. Possibly a million Jews died
in Jerusalem. The afterwards non-Jewish Christians came
to dominate the Christ-cult.

Christian communion represented on a silver paten, 3rd century A.D.

27   And he took the cup, and gave thanks, and gave it to them, saying, drink all of it, for this is my blood of the new testament, which is shed for many for the remission of sins.

35   And they crucified him, and parted his garments, casting lots, that it might be fulfilled as was spoken by the prophet: They parted my garments among them, and upon my robes they did cast lots.

36   And sitting down they watched him there

37   And set up over this head his accusation, written: this is Jesus, king of the Jews.

50   Jesus, when he had cried again with a loud voice, yielded up the ghost.

62   Now the next day, that followed the day of the preparation, the chief priests and Pharisees came together unto Pilate, saying we remember what that deceiver said, when alive: after three days I will rise again.

64   Command therefore that the grave be made sure until the third day, less his disciples come by night, steal him away, and say to the people: He is risen from the dead, so that the last error shall be worse than the first.

65   Pilate said unto them: You have a watch, go your way, make it as sure as you can.

66   So they went, and made the sepulchre sure, sealing the stone, and setting a watch.

No. 45. THERE IS POWER IN THE BLOOD.

L. E. J.

L. E. JONES.

1. Would you be free from your bur- den of sin? There's pow'r in the blood,
2. Would you be free from your passion and pride? There's pow'r in the blood,
3. Would you be whit- er, much whiter than snow? There's pow'r 'n the blood,
4. Would you do serv - ice for Jesus your King? There's pow'r in the blood,

pow'r in the blood; Would you o'er e - vil a vic- to- ry win?
pow'r in the blood; Come for a cleans- ing to Cal - va-ry's tide,
pow'r in the blood; Sin stains are lost in its life-giv- ing flow,
pow'r in the blood; Would you live dai - ly his prais - es to sing?

CHORUS.

There's won- der- ful pow'r in the blood. There is pow'r, pow'r,

There is pow'r,

wonder-working pow'r In the blood of the Lamb; There is

In the blood of the Lamb;

pow'r, pow'r, wonder-working pow'r In the precious blood of the Lamb.

There is pow'r,

Song from Christian Hymns No. 1, 1899, demonstrating the vampiric nature of the Christ-cult.

Chapter 28

2   And behold, there was a great earthquake, for the angel of the Lord descended from heaven, and came and rolled back the stone from the door, and sat upon it.

6   He is not here, for he is risen, as he said. Come, see the place where the Lord lay.

7   Go quickly, and tell his disciples that he is risen from the dead; and, behold, he goes before you into Galilee. There you will see him, as I have told you.

11   Now when they were going, behold, some of the watch came into the city, and showed to the chief priests all the things that were done.

12   And when they were assembled with the elders, and had taken counsel, they gave large money unto the soldiers, saying: Say his disciples came by night, and stole him away while we slept.

Gospel of Luke

Chapter 7

12   When he came to the gate of the city there was a dead man carried out, the only son of his mother, and she was a widow, and many of the people of the city were with her.

13   And when the Lord saw her, he had compassion on her, and said unto her: weep not.

A frieze from the 2nd century A.D., showing Christians
attacking Cybele riding a bull, with a Dionysian dance
taking place to the right. Several Roman Emperors
outlawed Christianity because of its intolerance and the
many murders committed by its followers.

14   And he came and touched the bier, and they that carried him stood still. And he said, Young man, I say unto thee, arise.

15   And he that was dead sat up, and began to speak. And Jesus delivered him to his mother.

34   The Son of man is come eating and drinking, and you say, behold a gluttonous man, and a wine drinker, a friend of publicans and sinners!

Chapter 8

52   And all wept, and bewailed her: but Jesus said weep not, she is not dead, but asleep.

53   And they laughed at him in scorn, knowing that she was dead.

54   He put them all out, and took her by the hand, and called saying, maid, arise.

55   And her spirit came again, and she arose straightway, and he commanded them to give her meat.

56   And her parents were astonished, but he charged them to tell no one.

Chapter 19

26   For I say unto you, that to every one which has shall be given more, and from those that have not, even what they have shall be taken from them.

27   But as to my enemies, which would not have me reign over them, bring them to me, and slay them before me.

28   And when Jesus had thus spoken he got up, and went up to Jerusalem.

Chapter 20

26   Show me a penny. Whose image and name does it bear? They answered and said, Caesar's.

27   And he said to them: render therefore to Caesar the things that are Caesars, and to God the things that are God's.

[given the generally pro-Roman and anti-Jewish tone of the Gospels, and that Caesar (either Tiberius or Gaius, depending on the date) had been proclaimed God, this is not simply an admonition to pay Roman taxes without complaint. It is a double emphatic: give to Caesar the things that are God's, because he is God.]

Gospel of John

Chapter 19

30   When Jesus therefore had received the vinegar, he said "It is finished" and he bowed his head and gave up the ghost.

31   The Jews, because it was the day of preparation for the Sabbath, so that the men not remain upon the crosses, asked Pilate that the victim's legs might be broken, and the corpses carried away.

THE TRIUMPH OF THE CHRIST CULT

4 B.C.	Date typically given for the birth of Jesus Christ.
29 A.D.	Date typically given for the death and resurrection of Jesus Christ.
70	Destruction of Jerusalem by Titus, who becomes Emperor in 79 A.D.
306	Constantine the Great becomes first Christian Emperor. Fighting among Christian sects intensifies; many labeled heretics and harassed or killed.
325	First Ecumenical Council at Nice, Bithynia.
300-400	About 1 million Arian Christians killed in war by Orthodox Christians.
379	Theodosius divides empire with Valentinian, burns temples of pagans, starts the Inquisition, which is used not only against pagans, but also against all Christian dissenters.
395	Roman empire breaks into pieces. Beginning of Dark Ages and Roman Catholic Church.
768-814	Rule of Charlemagne, Frankish Holy Roman Emperor. Successfully defends France from Islam, forces Christianity upon Saxons and others, killing some 2 million pagans.
1248	Crusade against Albigensian heretics in Southern France. Probably 2 million slaughtered, including women and children.
1492	Columbus claims Americas for Spain, begins the conversion and enslavement of the natives by Christians, a process that would lead to about 30 million deaths in the following 100 years. Inquisition re-established.
1500-	Christian Heretics begin to be able to defend themselves against the Catholic Church, and become known as Protestants, but only after millions of deaths in religious wars.
1600	Christianity has become the dominant world religion, with Roman Catholicism remaining its largest sect.

The vampire Jesus helping his soldiers slaughter innocent
pagans.

32   Then came the soldiers, and broke the legs of the first, and of the other who was crucified with him.

33   But when they came to Jesus, and saw that he was already dead, they did not break his legs.

34   But one of the soldiers with a spear pierced his side, and forthwith out came blood and water.

35   And he that saw this bore witness, and his witness is true; and he knows what he says is true, so that you might believe it.

The Acts of the Apostles

Chapter 14

19   And there came thither certain Jews from Antioch and Iconium, who persuaded the people, and, having stoned Paul, drew him out of the city, supposing he had been dead.

20   Howbeit, as the disciples stood round about him, he rose up, and came into the city: and the next day he departed with Barnabas to Derbe.

Second Epistle of Paul to the Thessalonians

Chapter 2

7   For the mystery of iniquity already works; only he who now allows it will allow it, until he be taken out of the way.

Jesus with two newly made immortals.

8   And then shall the Wicked be revealed, whom the Lord shall consume with the spirit of his mouth, and shall destroy with the brightness of his coming.

Chapter 3

1   Finally, brothers, pray for us, that the word of the Master may have free course, and be glorified, even as it is with you;

2   And that we may be delivered from unreasonable and wicked men, for all men have not faith.

3   But the Master is constant, who entombs you, and keeps you obedient.

4   We have confidence in the Master touching you, that you both do and will do the things which we command.

Revelations

Chapter 19

12   His eyes were as a flame of fire, and on his head were many crowns; and he had a name written, that no man knew, but he himself.

13   And he was clothed with a robe dipped in blood, and his name is called The Word of God.

15   And out of his mouth goes a sharp sword, that with it he should smite the nations, and he shall rule them with an iron rod, and tread the winepress of the fierceness and wrath of Almighty God.

Christian sarcophagus, where an immortal slept, with
picture of the Magi's offering gifts to Jesus at his
birth.

16   And he has on his clothing and on his thigh a name written, King of Kings and Lord of Lords.

[note this is the title which Gaius Caesar claimed for himself]

17   And I saw an angel standing in the sun, and he cried with a loud voice, saying to all the birds that fly in the air: come and gather yourselves together unto the supper of the great God.

18   That you may eat the flesh of kings and the flesh of captains, and the flesh of mighty men, and the flesh of horses, and of them that sit on them, and the flesh of all men, both free and slave, both small and great.

FURTHER READING

Ecclesiastical History by Eusebius

The Decline and Fall of the Roman Empire by Edward Gibbon

The True Authorship of the New Testament by Abelard Reuchlin

The Apostalic Fathers translated by Kirsopp Lake

Prudentius

Apollonius of Tyana, bust in the Capitoline Museum, Rome.
Apollonius healed the sick and cast out demons, but did
not claim to be god.

Apollonius of Tyana

Apollonius of Tyana does not fit our vampire-god criteria very well, but is included here to help paint a better picture of the wars between vampires and their zombie followers within the Roman Empire in the second and third centuries A.D. Apollonius of Tyana can be seen as a pagan Christ figure. Like Christ he was a holy man who performed a number of miracles, mainly healing the sick and casting out demons. However, Apollonius did not try to start a cult around himself. He concerned himself with the reform of the pagan cults that already existed, for instance arguing for substituting vegetable offerings for animal sacrifices.

Since he started no religion of his own he was not a serious rival to the Christians. Perhaps for that reason the major book on his life, Philostratus's The Life of Apollonius of Tyana, was preserved intact. However, this and other histories of Apollonius were used by Hierocles in his criticism of Christianity. Unfortunately Hierocles's actual essay was lost, except for parts of it quoted in the argument against it by the Christian bishop Eusebius (264-340 A.D.), which, if not totally convincing, adds great insight into the workings of the 3rd century Christian mindset. Eusebius felt it necessary to counter Philostratus and Hierocles because pagans were trying to show that many men had done what Jesus Christ had done, and therefore Christian claims to Jesus's divinity, and to being a universal and exclusive religion, were rather exaggerated. But if Eusebius had criticized the Gospels with the same arguments with which he criticized Philostratus's account, his fellow Christians would have had to burn him and his writings.

DOCUMENTS

The Life of Apollonius of Tyana

by Philostratus

Flavius Philostratus was a Greek professor around 170 A.D. These excerpts are based on the translation by F.C. Conybeare in 1912.

Book I, Chapter I

The votaries of Pythagoras of Samos have this story to tell of him [Pythagoras], that he was not an Ionian at all, but that, once on a time in Troy, he had been Euphobus, and that he had come to life after death, having died as the songs of Homer relate. And they say that he declined to wear apparel made from dead animal products and, to guard his purity, abstained from all flesh diet, and from the offering of animals in sacrifice. For that he would not stain the altars with blood; nay, rather the honey-cake and frankincense and the hymn of praise, these they say were the offerings made to the Gods by this man, who realized that they welcome such tribute more than they do the hecatombs and the knife laid upon the sacrificial basket. For they say that he certainly had social intercourse with the gods, and learned from them the conditions under which they take pleasure in men or are disgusted, and on this intercourse he based his account of nature. For he said that, whereas other men only make conjectures about the divinity and make guesses that contradict one another concerning it, in his own case he said that Apollo had come to him acknowledging that he was the god in person, and that Athena and the Muses and other gods, whose forms and names men did not yet know, had also consorted with him, though without making such acknowledgement.

...

For quite akin to theirs [the Pythagoreans] was the ideal which Apollonius pursued, and more divinely than Pythagoras he wooed wisdom and soared above tyrants. He lived in times not long gone by nor again quite of our own day, yet men know him not because of the true wisdom which he practiced as a sage and sanely. One man singles out one feature for praise in him and another a different feature, while some, because he had interviews with the wizards of Babylon and with the Brahmans of India, and with the nude ascetics of Egypt, put him down as a wizard, and spread the lie that he was a sage of an illegitimate kind, judging ill of him... It seems to me then that I ought not to condone or acquiesce in the general ignorance, but write a true account of the man, detailing the exact times at which he said or did this or that, as also the habits and temper of wisdom by means of which he succeeded in being considered a supernatural and divine being. And I have gathered my information partly from the many cities where he was loved, and partly from the temples of those long-neglected and decayed rites he restored, and partly from the accounts left of him by others and partly from his own letters. For he addressed these to kings, sophists, philosophers, to men of Elis, of Delphi, to Indians, and Egyptians; and his letters dealt with the subjects of the gods, of customs, of moral principles, of laws, and in all these departments he corrected the errors into which men had fallen. But the more precise details which I have collected are as follows.

Chapter XXX

Others say that he [Apollonius] died in Lindus, where he entered the temple of Athena and disappeared within it. Others again say that he died in Crete in a much more remarkable manner than the people of Lindus relate. For they say that he continued to live in Crete, where he became a greater center of admiration than ever before, and that he came to the temple of Dictynna late at night. Now this temple is guarded by dogs, whose duty it is to watch over the wealth deposited in it, and the Cretans claim that they are as good as bears or any other animals equally fierce. None the less, when he came, instead of barking, the approached him and fawned upon him, as they would not have done even with people they knew familiarly. The guardians of the shrine arrested him in consequence, and threw him in bonds as a wizard and a robber, accusing him of having thrown to the dogs some charmed morsel. But about midnight he loosened his bonds, and after calling those who had bound him, in order that they might witness the spectacle, he ran to the doors of the temple, which opened wide to receive him; and when he had passed within they closed afresh, as if they had been shut, and there was heard a chorus of maidens singing from within the temple and their song was this: "Hasten you from earth, hasten you to Heaven, hasten."

Chapter XXX in the Greek:

Οι δ εν Δινδω τελευτησαι αυτον, παρελθοντα ες το ιερον της Αθηνας και εσω αφανισθεντα οι δ εν Κρητη φασι Θαυμασιωτερον η οι εν Λινδω διατριβειν μεν γαρ εν τη Κρητη τον Απολλωνιον μαλλον η προ τουτον Θαυμαζομενον, αφικεσθαι δ εσ το ιερον της Δικτυννης αωρι. φνλακη δε τω ιερω κυνων επιτετακται, φρουροι τον εν αντω πλουτου, και αζιουσιν αυτους οι Κρητες μητε των αρκτων μητε των ωδε αγριων λειπεσθαι, οι δ ουθ υλακτειν ηκοντα σαινειν τε αντον προσιοντες, ως μηδε τους αγαν εθαδας. οι μεν δη του ιερου προισταμενοι ζυλλαβοντες αυτον ως γοητα και ληστην δησαι,

μειλιγμα τοις κυσι προβεβλησθαι τι υπ αυτου φασκοντες ο δ
αμφι μεσας νυκτας εαυτον λυσαι, καλεσας δε τους δησαντας, ως
μη λαθοι, δραμειν επι τας του ιερου θυρας, αι δ ανεπετασθησαν,
παρελθοντος δε εσω τας μεν θυρας ζυνελθειν, ωσπερ
εκεκλειντο, βοην δε αδουσων παρθενων εκπεσειν. το δε ασμα ην
στειχε γας, στειχε ες ουρανον, στειχε. οιον ιθι εκ της γης
αν ω.

Chapter XXXI

And even after his death he continued to preach that the
soul is immortal, but although he taught this account of it to be
correct, yet he discouraged men from meddling in such high
subjects.

Book IV, Chapter XLV

Here too is a miracle which Apollonius worked: a girl had
died just in the hour of her marriage, and the bridegroom was
following her bier lamenting her death. The whole of Rome
mourned with him, for the maiden belonged to a consular family.
Apollonius, witnessing their grief, said: "Put down the bier, for I
will stay the tears that you are shedding for this maiden." And he
asked her name. The crowd accordingly thought that he was about
to make an oration as is commonly delivered as much to grace the
funeral as to stir up lamentation; but he did nothing of the kind,
merely touching her and whispering in secret some spell over her.
She at once woke up from her seeming death; and the girl spoke
out loud, and returned to her father's house, just as Alcestis did
when she was brought back to life by Hercules. And the relations
of the maiden wanted to present him with the sum of 150,000

172

sesterces, but he said that he would freely present the money to the young lady by way of a dowry. Now whether he detected some spark of life in her, which those who were nursing her had not noticed — for it is said that although it was raining at the time, a vapour went up from her face — or whether life was really extinct, and he restored it with the warmth of his touch, is a mysterious problem which neither I myself nor those who were present could decide.

Book III, Chapter XXXIX

There also arrived a man who was lame. He was already thirty years old and was a keen hunter of lions; but a lion had sprung upon him and dislocated his hip so that he limped. However, when Apollonius massaged with his hands the youth's hip, he immediately recovered his upright gait. And another man had had his eyes put out, and he went away having recovered the sight of both of them. Yet another man had his hand paralyzed, but left their presence in full possession of the limb. And a certain woman had suffered in labour already seven times, but was healed in the following way through the intercession of her husband. He bade the man, whenever his wife should be about to bring forth her next child, to enter her chamber carrying in his bosom a live hare. Then he was to walk once round her and at the same moment to release the hare; for that the womb would be extruded together with the foetus, unless the hare was at once driven out.

Book II, Chapter XIV

And Apollonius saw a herd of about thirty elephants crossing over the River Indus, and they were following as their leader the smallest among them. The bigger ones had picked up their young ones on their projecting tusks, where they held them fast by twining their trunks around them. Said Apollonius: "No one, O

Damis, has instructed them to do this, but they act of their own instinctive wisdom and cleverness. You see how, like porters, they have picked up their young, and have them bound fast on, and so carry them along."

"I see," he said, "Apollonius, how cleverly and with what sagacity they do this. What then is the sense of the silly speculation indulged in by those who idly dispute whether or not the affection that men feel for their young is natural or not, when these very elephants, by their conduct, proclaim that it is so, and that it comes to them by nature? For they have certainly not learned to do so from men, as have other creatures; for these have never yet shared the life of men, but have been endowed by nature with their love of their offspring, and that is why they provide for them and feed their young."

"And," said Apollonius, "you need not, Damis, confine your remarks to elephants; for this animal is only second to man, in my opinion, in understanding and foresight; but I am thinking rather of bears, for they are the fiercest of all animals, and yet they will do anything for their cubs; and also of wolves, among which, although they are so addicted to plunder, yet the female protects its young ones, and the male brings her food in order to save the life of the whelps... And if we look at creatures in the sea, we need not wonder at the dolphins loving their offspring, for they are superior creatures; but shall we not admire the whales and seals and the viviparous species? For I once saw a seal that was kept shut up at Aegae in the circus, and she mouned so deeply for her whelp, which had died after being born in confinement, that she refused food for three days together, although she is the most voracious of animals.

The Treatise of Eusebius, the Son of Pamphilus,
Against the Life of Apollonius of Tyana
Written by Philostratus, Occasioned by the Parallel
Drawn by Hierocles between Apollonius and Christ

Chapter II

I need not say with what admiring approval he [Hierocles] attributes Apollonius's magic feats not to the tricks of wizardry, but to a divine and mysterious wisdom. He believes they were truly what he supposes them to have been, though he advances no proof of his contention. Listen then to his very words: "In their anxiety to exalt Jesus, they run up and down prating of how he made the blind to see and worked certain other miracles of the kind." Then after an interval he adds as follows: "Let us note, however, how much better and more sensible is the view which we take of such matters, and explain the conception which we entertain of men gifted with remarkable powers." And thereupon after passing heedlessly by Aristeas of Proconnesus and Pythagoras as somewhat too old, he continues thus: "But in the time of our own ancestors, during the reign of Nero, there flourished Apollonius of Tyana, who from mere boyhood when he became the priest in Aegae of Cilicia of Aselepius, the lover of mankind, worked any number of miracles, of which I will omit the greater number and only mention a few." Then he begins at the beginning and enumerates the wonders worked by Apollonius, after which he continues in the following words: "What then is my reason for mentioning these facts? It was in order that you may be able to contrast our own accurate and well-established judgement on each point, with the easy gullibility of the Christians. For whereas we reckon him who wrought such feats not a god, but only a man pleasing to the gods, they on the strength of a few miracles proclaim their Jesus a god." To this he adds after a little more the following remark: "And this point is also worth noticing, that whereas the tales of Jesus have been vamped up by Peter and Paul and a few others of the kind — men who were liars and wizards and devoid of education — the history of Apollonius was written by Maximus of Aegae, and by Damis the philosopher who lived constantly with him, and by Philostratus of Athens, men of the highest education, who out of respect for the truth and their love of mankind determined to give the publicity they deserved to the actions of a man at once noble and a friend of the gods." These are the very words used by Hierocles in his treatise against us which he had entitled "Lover of Truth."

FURTHER READING

The Life of Apollonius of Tyana by Philostratus

Lao Tzu, born 604 B.C., the author of the Tao Te Ching, who disappeared without a trace.

CHANG LING AND THE TAOISTS

In Western China, in the same century during which Jesus Christ, Gaius Caesar, and Quetzalcoatl lived, another new religion was founded by another man who claimed to be immortal: Chang Ling. He is often called the Pope of Taoism, and his lineage ruled a religious empire until the founding of the Chinese Republic in this century.

Taoism existed before Chang Ling, but probably not as an organized, hierarchical religion. Its chief document was the Tao Te Ching — The Way and Its Power, attributed to Lao Tzu (b. 604 B.C.). Its adherents sought mystical experience. But its followers had other wants, too, and were much involved in alchemy, seeking an elixir of immortality. Claims have been made that several, perhaps many Taoists besides Chang Ling achieved immense age or immortality. The writings of Kwang Tze (or Chuang Tzu), who lived from about 369 to 286 B.C., mentions one Phang Tzu, who obtained the Tao in the time of Shun, and lived on to the time of the five leading princes of Kau, a total of more than 1800 years. Then there was Kwang Khang Tze, who instructed king Hwang Ti in the year 2679 B.C., and claimed that year to be 1200 years old, giving him a birth year of 3879 B.C.

Chang Ling is said to have been a scholar born 35 A.D. One day he exclaimed: "What can literature do to prolong life?" He then sought to use alchemy to prepare an immortality drug. After long study and experimentation he succeeded in properly mixing the "blue dragon" with the "white tiger," and was thereupon able to make a pill of immortality. Though he was 60 years old, he looked like a youth after taking the pill.

Kwang Tze, 12th century A.D. representation. Though his and other Taoist writings were apparently anti-authoritarian, Taoism was instituted by Chang Ling in the first century A.D. as a hierarchical, authoritarian religion as oppressive as any in the world.

His fame grew and he became an expert at healing. However, he charged for this services five bushels of rice per sick person. The peasants thereby nicknamed him Mitsei, or Rice-thief. The number of his disciples grew to over ten thousand, so he established a hierarchy to rule over them. This became a quasi-state; he commanded the people to build roads and bridges and do other tasks. The punishment for refusal was sickness.

Chang Ling lived on earth until 157 A.D., at which time he assembled his followers and ascended into heaven before their eyes.

DOCUMENTS

Tao Te Ching

by Lao Tzu

Verse 33

He who knows other men is discerning;
He who knows himself is intelligent.
He who overcomes others is strong;
He who overcomes himself is mighty.
He who is satisfied with his lot is rich;
He who goes on acting with energy has a will.
He who does not fail in the requirements
of his position, continues long;
He who dies and yet does not perish,
Has longevity.

Verse 50

Men come forth and live;
They enter and die.
Of every ten three administer life to themselves;
and three administer death.
There are also three in every ten whose aim is life,
but whose movements tend to the land of death.
And for what reason?
Because of their excessive endeavors to perpetuate life.

But I have heard that he who is skillful in managing his life
for a time travels on the land
without having to shun rhinoceros or tiger.
He enters an opposing army
without having to avoid armor or sword.
The rhinoceros finds no place in him
into which to thrust its horn,
Nor the tiger a place in which to fix its claws,
Nor the weapon a place to admit its edge.

And for what reason?
Because in him there is no place of death.

The Writings of Kwang Tze

Chapter 6

7   This is the Tao. There is in it emotion and sincerity, but it does nothing and has no bodily form. It may be handed down, but may not be received. It may be apprehended, but it cannot be seen. It has its root and ground of existence in itself. Before there were heaven and earth, from of old, there it was, securely existing.

From it came the mysterious existences of spirits, from it the mysterious existence of God. It produced heaven; it produced earth. It was before the primal ether, and yet could not be considered high. It was below all space, and yet could not be considered deep. It was produced before heaven and earth, and yet could not be considered to have existed long. It was older than the oldest antiquity, and yet could not be considered old.

Shih-wei got it, and by it adjusted heaven and earth. Fu-hsi got it, and by it penetrated to the mystery of the maternity of the primary matter. The Big Dipper got it, and from all antiquity has made no eccentric movement. The Sun and Moon got it, and from all antiquity have not stopped shining. Khan-pei got it, and by it became lord of Khwan-lun. Fang-i got it, and by it enjoyed himself in the Great River. Kien Wu got it, and by it dwelt on mount Thai. Hwant Ti got it, and by it ascended the cloudy sky. Kwan Hsu got it, and by it dwelt in the Dark Palace. Yu-hiagn got it, and by it was set on the North Pole. Hsi Wang Mu got it, and by it had her seat in the palace of Shao-kwang. No one knows its beginning; no one knows its end. Phang Tzu got it, and lived on from the time of the Lord of Yu to that of the Five Chiefs. Fu Yueh got it, and by it became chief minister to Wu-ting, who thus became master of the kingdom. Fu-Yueh mounted to the eastern portion of the Milky Way, where, riding on Sagittarius and Scorpio, he took his place among the stars.

Chapter 11

4   Hwang-Ti had been on the throne for nineteen years and his ordinances were in operation all through the kingdom, when he heard that Kwang Khang Tze was living on the summit of Khung-thung, and went to see him. 'I have heard' he said, 'that you, Sir, and well acquainted with the perfect Tao. I venture to ask you what is the essential thing in it. I wish to take the subtlest

influences of heaven and earth, and assist with them the growing of the five cereals for the better nourishment of the people. I also wish to direct the operation of the Yin and Yang, so as to secure the comfort of all living beings. How shall I proceed to accomplish those objects?'

Kwang Khang Tze replied, 'What you wish to ask about is the original substance of all things; what you to have the direction of is that substance as it was shattered and divided. According to your government of the world, the vapors of the clouds, before they were collected, would descend in rain; the herbs and trees would shed their leaves before they became yellow; and the light of the sun and moon would hasten to extinction. Your mind is that of a flatterer with his plausible words; it is not fit that I should tell you the perfect Tao.'

Hwang Ti withdrew, gave up his kingdom, built himself a solitary apartment, spread in it a mat of the white mao grass, dwelt in it unoccupied for three months, and then went again to seek an interview. Kwang Khang Tze was then lying down with his head to the south. Hwang Ti, with an air of deferential submission, went forward on his knees, twice bowed low with his face to the ground, and asked him, saying, 'I have heard that you, Sir, are well acquainted with the perfect Tao. I venture to ask how I should rule my body, in order that it may continue for a long time.'

Kwang Khang Tze hastily rose, and said, 'A good question! Come and I will tell you the perfect Tao. Its essence is the deepest obscurity; its highest reach is in darkness and silence. There is nothing to be seen; nothing to be heard. When it holds the spirit in its arms in stillness, then the bodily form of itself will become correct. You must be still; you must be pure; not subjecting your body to toil, not agitating your vital force; then you may live for long. When your eyes see nothing, your ears hear nothing, and your mind knows nothing, your spirit will keep your body, and the body will live long. Watch over what is within you, shut up the avenue that connect you with what is external; much knowledge is pernicious. I proceed with you to the summit of the Grand Brilliance, where we come to the source of the bright and expanding element. I will enter with you the gate of the Deepest Obscurity, where we come to the source of the dark and repressing. There heaven and earth have their controllers; their Yin and Yang have their Repositories. Watch over and keep your body, and all things will of themselves give it vigor. I maintain the unity, and dwell in harmony. In this way I have cultivated myself for one thousand and two hundred years, and my body form has undergone no decay.

184

DRACULA

Bram Stoker's novel *Dracula* defined vampires for our epoch. Trying to draw facts out of a partially fictional work is a labor prone to error.

Most people today don't believe in vampires. Vampires are merely a fiction, something to scare and thrill children and paranoids. And if anything, post-Stoker vampires have descended into complete parody, with the sucking of blood the essential element.

Anyone can cut someone's throat with a knife, sharp nails, or teeth and drink human blood. It doesn't make anyone immortal. Yet everyday thousands of people are saved by blood transfusions.

Much has been made of Stoker's Dracula as a parable for sexual eroticism. Certainly sexuality was repressed or at best alluded to in most of the literature of the period. Yet the absence of overt sexuality hardly stands as proof that sexuality is essential to a novel. Like clever magicians, academic pontificators have sought to draw the public eye away from the central story: real people encountering and fighting a real vampire.

In Stoker's Dracula five men oppose the undead Count: Jonathan Harker, a lawyer experienced in words but not reality; Dr. Seward, a psychiatrist (alienist was the term used back then) and caretaker of mad people; Quincey Morris, an American, representing men of action; Arthur Holmwood, Lucy's fiancee; and Abraham Van Helsing, a scientist (and likely not a christian).

Today most scientists scoff at vampires; and doubtless they did in 1897 as well. But a scientist is simply someone who has passed a course in science and sucked up to someone who passed a similar course some years earlier; a man who might know, perhaps, everything about the hind legs of ants but no more than is ordinary about everything else.

Van Helsing knew about vampires. Ordinary people did not, apparently, except perhaps in Transylvania. How did Van Helsing know about vampires? We are not told. How did Stoker know about vampires? We are not told. Were there literary predecessors to Dracula? And what were Stoker's sixteen other books?

Bram Stoker was well schooled at Trinity College; almost certainly he read the same Greek and Roman classics that are examined here. He grew up in Dublin, where Catholic superstitions were accepted as fact. Perhaps he put the facts together subconsciously in writing Dracula; perhaps he consciously put those facts together; and perhaps someone who had actual knowledge of vampires set him on the right course. It is reported that his mother told him stories of ghosts and perhaps vampires, but we don't know the details. Likely we will never know.

Once science became a cult or social movement its followers largely rejected conventional religions in favor of rationalism and its attendant Atheism or Deism (belief in God the totally uncaring). It prided itself in rejecting superstition, including the Christian superstitions prevalent in Europe. Thus Jesus Christ, it was thought, could not have risen from the dead anymore than Dionysus or Osiris or Dracula could have.

Stoker gave very little background about Dracula in his novel. Could he have chosen Dracula as a symbol? Certainly. Dracula could have symbolized almost anything: "immoral" impulses suppressed by society, vampires in general, or as George Stade says in his Introduction to the Bantam Classic edition of Dracula, he could be a stand in for Jesus Christ.

Medieval and Renaissance scientists were locked in a titanic battle with the Catholic Church, and the battle is still being waged. For instance teaching Darwin's Theory of Evolution was banned by many churches at the time Stoker wrote. Could some scientists have known about vampires, and passed that knowledge down until it eventually reached Stoker, who wanted to popularize it?

Still, why Dracula? Did Stoker simply pick this historical figure out of air, or was the former Prince of Wallachia (the fertile area of Western Romania between Transylvania and the Danube) already figuring as a vampire in legends? Why was the belief in vampires common among slavic peoples, including those inhabiting Transylvania?

Symbols here, symbols there, symbols, symbols everywhere. Unless Dracula was based on a true story. And, of course, most people who have done a bit of research admit that Dracula was the name of a historic figure who lived from 1431 to 1476, also known as Vlad the Impaler.

History records were not kept in Dracula's Wallachia. Before Dracula we do not even have a reliable record of the descent of the Princes of Wallachia. What scant records there are, are from neighboring kingdoms that were less anarchistic. However, with some certainty we know that Mircea the Old established himself as Prince of Wallachia, and that at his death his sons contested for the throne. Both Dan II and Radu the Bald are believed to have ruled for a time, followed by Vlad, who ascended in 1436. The people of Wallachia weren't real keen on government generally, and Vlad had to massacre a lot of his subjects to terminate a peasant revolt in 1438.

However, from Vatican records we know that in 1431 Vlad joined the Order of the Dragon, and it was the Vatican's support that helped Vlad finally gain the thrown. Someone decided to nickname Vlad Dracul, the native word for Dragon, and he accepted the name.

Those were turbulent times; Christianity was still losing its war with the Moslems, represented in eastern Europe by the Turks, who had a major interest in Wallachia. Dracul was deposed and then reinstated, only to be killed in 1447 by the knight Hunyady, who was Regent of Hungary, which ruled over Transylvania and was constantly at war with the Turks. Vlad's son Vlad III, also known as Dracula, had been born in 1431 and was only 16 when his father died. The thrown of Wallachia again was contested, and in 1448 Dracula held it for one month before being deposed.

In 1456 Dracula was finally made Prince of Wallachia by Hunyady, who died of the plague the same year. Hunyady, it should be said, was a Catholic, and so was Dracula. His countrymen, however, were mostly either pagans or Eastern Orthodox. Dracula gradually became more powerful, and like Draco of Athens two millennia earlier made death the penalty for almost all offenses. In 1458, at Easter, he slaughtered the nobles and knights of his country who opposed him. This unchivalrous act made Dracula feared in his own kingdom and known throughout Europe. That same year Dracula refused to pay tribute to the Turks. His bloodthirst knew no bounds; the countryside was littered with men, and women and children, impaled on stakes.

In 1461 Dracula began attacking the Turkish possessions in eastern Europe; Pope Pius II hoped he would play the same role against the Moslem Turks that the Kings of Castile were playing against the Spanish Moslems. But instead the Turks invaded Wallachia the following year and placed Dracula's brother Radu on the thrown. Dracula then lived in exile — really prison — in Hungary until 1474, when he was allowed freedom in return for rallying Wallachia against the Turks again. He was supposed killed on the battlefield in 1476. Yet either his memory or his ghost — or himself, a vampire — continued to haunt the peasants of Wallachia and neighboring Transylvania.

If there is a symbol in Stoker's Dracula, it is the sucking of blood from mortal humans. It stands for the ability, the need, of the ancient immortals to sup on the vitality of men and women. Which may even be a mistaken belief. True, vampires set up and controlled cults large and small, but so have mere mortals. Possibly immortality is a given for vampires: they will be immortal no matter how they act. But some, at least, like power over other men, a trait easy enough to understand without resorting to mysticism.

Stoker's Dracula sleeps in the day, parties at night, and can appear as a substantial human being or in any number of insubstantial forms. Most of the vampires discussed in this book share these abilities.

There are persistent rumors that the real Vlad Dracula did not die in 1476. Instead he became an important figure in the Catholic Church, and an effective director of the Inquisition, which was directed primarily against Jews, Protestants, and the growing rationalism of the scientists.

1476 was a bit late to declare oneself a god; better to be a powerful figure in an established, powerful cult. A mere 16 years the man Dracula worshipped — Jesus Christ — would finally be able to take center stage in the world, partly due to the technological discoveries of the very scientists who opposed his church.

FURTHER READING

Dracula, A Biography of Vlad the Impaler 1431-1476 by Radu Florescu and Raymond T. McNally

History of the Roumanians by R.W. Seton-Watson

Bibliography

[see also the works listed under Further Reading at the end of most chapters]

World Religions From Ancient History to the Present, edited by Geoffrey Parrinder

The World's Sixteen Crucified Saviors by Kersey Graves [available from Loompanics, Unlimited, P.O. Box 1197, Port Townsend, WA 98368]

The Decline and Fall of the Roman Empire by Edward Gibbon

The Loeb Classic series. Virtually everything written in the Classic Roman world that has survived is available in this series, which features the Greek or Latin text side by side with translations. You can get a catalog of the complete series by requesting it from Harvard University Press, 79 Garden Street, Cambridge, MA 02138 USA

Other books of interest from III Publishing

Fiction:

The Last Days of Christ the Vampire by J.G. Eccarius

The satire classic that broke the silence about the vampiric nature of Jesus Christ and his fundamentalist zombies. Jesus has set his sights on converting some teenagers in Providence, Rhode Island, but instead they resist and set out to hunt him down before he can release his Apocalypse upon the world. Jesus Lives; vampires never die.

Virgintooth by Mark Ivanhoe

There is no escape: at death every soul is swallowed up into the abysmal hunger of the feral vampires. Elizabeth, however, has not exactly died: she has been made. Now she has not only the problems she had when alive, and of avoiding the feral vampires, but she must also get along with the other human vampires. At times terrifying, at times hysterically funny, Virgintooth will enlighten and delight you.

Geminga, Sword of the Shining Path by Melvin Litton

In a world poised between a superstitious past and a surreal future of bioengineering, virtual reality and artificial consciousness, Geminga surfs on the winds of the present. A product of genetic engineering, this bird has been trained since infancy to assassinate the enemies of Peru's Sendero Luminoso. Now she's come with her best friend, Jimmy the Snake, to California Norte.

This'll Kill Ya by Harry Willson

The Anti-censorship thriller that will have you laughing out loud and examining your own reactions to materials that surely should be censored. Caution: If you believe that words can be used as weapons to harm people, reading these pages may be hazardous to your health. Willson has a devilishly delightful sense of humor that should place him in everyone's home library.

We Should Have Killed the King by J.G. Eccarius

Jack Straw and hundreds of thousands of other English peasants rebelled against their overlords in 1381, killing nobles, lawyers and tax collectors. Ultimately they were crushed, but the spirit of rebellion was reborn in America in the punk/anarchist movement during the 1980's and Jack Straw was there. A stunning look at the underground in the USA.

Available at bookstores not run by zombies.

To order direct from III Publishing send $8.00 per book (postage included) to III Publishing, P.O. Box 170363, San Francisco, CA 94117-0363

Index

192